DAVON B. CAMP

STUTTERING TO THE TOP

ELOHAI
INTERNATIONAL
PUBLISHING & MEDIA

Print ISBN: 978-1-953535-15-3

eBook ISBN: 978-1-953535-57-3

Published by ELOHAI International Publishing & Media

P.O. Box 1883

Cypress, TX 77410

hello@elohaiintl.com

elohaiintl.com

This book is dedicated to anyone who has ever dealt with
self-doubt, self-hatred, and lack of confidence.
May you accept the power to silence the negative voice,
empower the positive voice, and unconditionally love yourself
to unleash your true potential so you can achieve
whatever your heart desires.

Acclaim for Stuttering to the Top

"The words written within this book are captivating. I was quite literally transported into this emotional memoir and felt every anxious moment, each frustration, every hurt, the anguish, and the invocation of tears when victory was achieved. You are left with no choice but to feel with DaVon as he shares his truth and pours his pain and healing into each page of his personal story and the insecurities he has faced."

—Joseph Snider, LCSW-C, LICSW, Therapist and Author

"*Stuttering to the Top* is an inspiring and captivating read. In this book, DaVon opens up about his life journey, navigating the challenges of living with a stutter. This book is a testament to resilience and self-discovery, making it a must-read for anyone seeking motivation and understanding."

—Danny Prince II, Author, Teen Pastor, Speaker

"This insightful and introspective exploration takes readers on a journey into the profound impact of a person who stutters' inner voice on their actions and reactions in daily life. The author is refreshingly vulnerable and authentic as he shares how his perspective evolved over time—from a young boy who stutters to a confident, successful father raising a son who also stutters."

—Timothy Flynn, Speech-Language Pathologist, National Stuttering Association DC Co-Chapter Leader

"*Stuttering to the Top* is an inspiring story that illuminates the power of resilience to achieve personal and professional success. Through a blend of candid anecdotes and vulnerable insights, the book offers a powerful message about embracing one's unique qualities and defying societal pressures. It's a motivating read for anyone who has faced adversity and negative self-efficacy, bringing a renewed and refreshing perspective to the transformation of self-doubt to self-confidence …"

—Aidan Marshall-Cort, Researcher, National Stuttering Association DC Co-Chapter Leader and Mid-Atlantic Coordinator

Contents

CHAPTER 1

The Beginning and the Diagnosis (He Stutters)

I was born in September of 1984, at Columbia Hospital in Washington, DC, and grew up in the Northeast quadrant of the city. The neighborhood where I lived for a lot of my childhood was Brentwood/Saratoga within the Brookland Manor Apartment Complex.

This apartment complex has roots that run deep in DC and is widely known as a historically black community that has housed multi-generational families since the late 1930s. Brookland Manor is one of the largest affordable housing complexes in DC. Although this area has deep roots, it was notorious for crime and drugs in the 1980s and 1990s and still is today.

I was raised by a fourteen-year-old mother and my grandmother, who I affectionately called "Ma." My grandmother made it clear when I started talking that she was too young to be called "Grandma."

At the time of my birth, we lived in a small apartment where I was lovingly cared for by the women in my life. While my mother finished high school, we lived with my grandmother who helped raise me, along with her son, (my uncle), who was only two years older than me. Even growing up in low-income housing, which some would consider the "ghetto", I never felt poor. I had everything I needed.

The internet didn't become available until 1993 and I didn't get the opportunity to use it until my sophomore year in high school in 1999. Naturally, it still wasn't used like it is today with multiple social media platforms.

Therefore, I had nothing to compare my environment to. My friends and I were pretty much on an even playing field as it related to our socioeconomic status. My father was incarcerated shortly after I was born, but his mother and stepfather, my grandparents, also stepped in to help raise and provide for me.

My family members said I started to stutter when I was a toddler. They said I was energetic and full of life. Sometimes my energetic personality would lead to broken items around the apartment. Once I entered into pre-kindergarten, it was very evident that I stuttered. At seven years old and in second grade, my mother and grandmother took me to have a speech evaluation by a speech and language specialist and I was officially diagnosed as a person who stutters.

The National Institute on Deafness and Other Communication Disorders defines stuttering as "a speech disorder characterized by repetition of sounds, syllables, or words; prolongation of sounds; and interruptions in speech known as blocks. An individual who stutters knows exactly what he or she would like to say but has trouble producing a normal flow of speech.

"These speech disruptions may be accompanied by struggle behaviors, such as rapid eye blinks or tremors of the lips."[1]

The exact cause of stuttering is unknown, however there is a lot of research, and most experts agree that stuttering has a neurological basis, affecting areas of the brain that control how speech and language are processed.

As it relates to the causes of stuttering The National Stuttering Association states "The precise causes of stuttering are still unknown, but most researchers now consider stuttering to involve differences in brain activity that interfere with the production of speech. In some people, the tendency to stutter may be inherited.

"The most common type of stuttering (sometimes called developmental stuttering) usually develops in childhood, most often between ages two and eight (although in rare cases

---

1   https://www.nidcd.nih.gov/health/stuttering#what

it may begin much later). Roughly 4 to 5 percent of people experience stuttering at some time during their childhood."[2]

I remember that first speech evaluation like it was yesterday. The speech pathologist was so nice. The evaluation consisted of a series of questions that I had to answer. I remember having to read out loud and I commented, "I don't usually stutter when I read." I was so frustrated because I wanted to be fluent. I didn't want to stutter.

The speech pathologist was being very patient with me as I grew more frustrated and she said, "It's ok if you stutter." It didn't dawn on me then, as I battled with frustration during this evaluation, but I would later realize I should have really listened to this woman because those few words are so powerful—it's ok if you stutter. I would not hear them again for over twenty-five years.

My mom opted to not explore speech therapy for me. Many people believed I could "grow out" of my stutter because there had been success stories of other people who came before me that grew out of their stutter.

When I became an adult, my grandmother, who is now deceased, and who was at the evaluation when I was diagnosed as a person who stutters, stated she wished they had

---

2   https://westutter.org/what-is-stuttering/

explored speech therapy for me because she "could see it on my face, that even as an adult, it still bothered me."

CHAPTER 2

The Class Clown

Early on, after my diagnosis, I had days when I wished my stutter was like a bad headache, and that I could "sleep it away" and after a good night's rest, my stutter would be gone. But that never happened. I had many days where I asked myself, "Why me? I don't understand." I would also ask myself, "Why don't any of the other kids stutter?" I only knew one person who stuttered. It was an elderly great-grandparent on my father's side of the family who passed away when I was young.

It was difficult for me during kindergarten through second grade. My classmates asked me, "Why do you talk like that?" Some were genuinely concerned because I exhibited struggling behaviors while speaking. Stomping my foot, or feet, or rolling my eyes in the back of my head while trying to speak are examples of struggling behaviors.

While some classmates were concerned, other classmates were rude, as some would greet me in the morning with,

"What's up DaDaDaDaDaVon?" as a way of making fun of my stuttering but not understanding the impact it had on me mentally, at a very fragile age.

In second grade, I remember every student had to stand up and share what they wanted to be when they grew up. When it came to my turn, I said, "A lawyer." Several of my classmates burst out in laughter. One classmate shouted, "How are you going to be a lawyer? You don't even talk straight."

Instead of saying something rude back, I sat down in my seat, and thought about the lawyer movies I had seen; remembering how they have to stand up and do a lot of talking in court to help people who are in trouble. My classmate was right. I couldn't do that. Here I was, eight years old, thinking to myself, "Pretty much every job requires you to talk. I won't be able to do anything when I grow up because I stutter."

It was at this point when I decided to take on the role of class clown. I figured it would take some of the attention away from my stutter if I was the funny guy. Unfortunately, that didn't go so well with my teacher. My classmates definitely enjoyed the laughs. My teacher would call my mom and complain, and my mom did not tolerate any nonsense at school.

Education was very important to my mom, and she required that I take it seriously. But what she didn't know was being the class clown was an outlet; I was struggling with my stutter but didn't know how to communicate that to her.

The class clown tag would follow me throughout grade school. It was all I had at the time to cope with my stutter. I wanted people to laugh with me and not at me.

———

Although we didn't talk about stuttering in the household, my mom never allowed me to make it a crutch. I grew up in a Christian household and going to church was very much a part of my childhood. My mom would make me speak in church and participate in church events. I remember one event in particular. I was probably nine years old when my mom signed me up to be on the church's step team.

We were required to learn a step routine, and I was also asked to do a gospel rap routine during the performance. I was so nervous. I asked myself, "Why would they ask the kid who stutters to rap?" Although I never communicated my fear of this performance to my mother, she helped me prepare. We practiced and practiced some more. When it came time to perform, I knew my step routine and the lyrics they wanted me to rap, but was so nervous that I would stutter.

Here we were, the day of the performance, and it was time. It was a very sunny and humid day, and the performance was outside in the church's parking lot. I had all the signs: forehead hot from the sun shining, heart racing, and upset stomach. I was nervous. Many people came to the performance.

We started the performance with the step routine, and then they gave me the signal to start my gospel rap. My heart was racing, but I locked in. I said my rap as I rehearsed 1,000 times and I got through it. This was my first out-of-body experience. I can't remember how much I stuttered, but I got through it. It felt so good. I loved the feeling of executing the performance, but I hated the preparation and the fear of stuttering in front of a group of people.

Stuttering was not the issue; it was the fear of stuttering and how everyone else would react to my stutter that I didn't like. But again, I was not comfortable with my stutter at this point in my life. I didn't even feel comfortable saying the word "stutter." I cringed at the thought of being a person who stutters. I hated it with a passion. My goal was to do everything possible to become a fluent speaker.

CHAPTER 3

Joining

In 1991, a movie was released in theaters titled *New Jack City*. It was an American crime action film based on an original story. The plot followed the character Nino Brown, a drug kingpin, in New York City during the crack epidemic. American Actor Wesley Snipes played in this role. There was another character in the movie named the "Duh Duh Duh Man" who acquired this nickname because of his stutter and was a personal bodyguard and enforcer for Nino Brown. American actor Bill Nunn, who died in 2016 from leukemia, played in this role.

Ironically, growing up and to this day, that is one of my favorite movies. But when it was released, I was regularly called the Duh Duh Duh Man. It became one of my nicknames, which I hated with a passion. I had never really seen anyone stutter, and I never looked in the mirror to see how I stuttered, so the Duh Duh Duh Man was my only visual of how stuttering looked.

He exhibited struggling behaviors when he spoke in the movie, and I knew I exhibited the same behaviors because I felt them when I spoke. Silently I told myself, "I see why people laugh or ask 'what's wrong with me.' When people stutter, it's either concerning or funny; there's no in between." This movie made me hate myself even more because now that I saw what I looked like when I stuttered, it was embarrassing.

Another key movie came out in 1994, *Forrest Gump*. It was an American comedy-drama film and adaptation of the 1986 novel of the same name. The film followed an Alabama man named Forrest Gump, played by American actor Tom Hanks, and his experiences as a person with a physical disability and low intelligence.

There was a particular scene in the movie that took place when Forrest Gump was in grade school. He waited for the bus one morning on the first day of school. After getting on the bus, he walked down the aisle looking for a seat. Much to his dismay, he was greeted with unkind words from mean kids, "seats taken" and "can't sit here."

A young lady, who would later become Forrest Gump's wife in the movie, said, "You can sit here if you want," and he sat down beside her. Noticing Forrest wore braces, she proceeded to ask him about his physical disability and discovered they were for correcting his curved spine. She then looked at him and asked, "Are you stupid or something?"

Forrest Gump responded, "Mama says 'stupid is as stupid does,'" and they continued to talk.

When this movie was released, some people started calling me Forrest Gump because they related stuttering to a lack of intelligence which was so far from the truth.

The Raising Children Network states "Preschoolers might not be aware of their stuttering, and stuttering won't affect their development. Preschoolers who stutter can have the same social skills as non-stuttering children. Your child isn't more likely to be shy or withdrawn compared with children their age who don't stutter. But **if stuttering continues into primary school**, it can become a problem.

"If your child stutters, they might feel frustrated or embarrassed because of the way other children react to the way they speak. Your child might avoid talking or change what they want to say to avoid stuttering. They might not want to join in with classroom discussions.

"Primary school-age children are less likely to be thought of as leaders by their peers and more likely to be bullied compared with children who don't stutter.

"Teenagers who stutter can develop stress or anxiety because of their stuttering. They might feel self-conscious, have lower self-esteem or find some situations challenging—for example, speaking in public or starting an intimate relationship."[3]

The Urban Dictionary defines Joning as "making fun of a person to the point where they laugh uncontrollably."[4] In DC, joning was a regular part of my early teenage years. Once I entered middle school, I developed a tough exterior and started defending myself against people who weaponized my stuttering to tease me. I would find issues or deficiencies with them and use that to respond back to their comments about my stuttering. Now, at this point in my life, I didn't feel as though I was being targeted because of my stutter because no one was off limits in my neighborhood. Everyone got joned on, it was just that my particular thing was stuttering.

Some people got joned on because they had big lips, a big head, big feet, a scar on their face, etc. It did not matter. Yes, it bothered me that my stutter was the focus all the time, but I would jone back and never feared getting laughed at. We would stand outside on the corner of Saratoga Ave and 14th Street or hang out at the Brookland Manor Boys and Girls

---

3   https://raisingchildren.net.au/preschoolers/development/language-development/stuttering

4   https://www.urbandictionary.com/define.php?term=Joning

Club, where I spent a lot of time and jone on each other all the time.

We would jone and have fun for hours, but sometimes the joning would cause fighting because not everyone liked it, but the difference between kids fighting now and us fighting back in the 1990s, is that we would fight and the next day we were back friends. Now with social media things go viral causing embarrassment which leads to unwanted violence.

I think back to this time and realize it's when I became more resilient. I didn't shy away from talking completely, but I did have moments when it would bother me when people would finish a sentence for me or would tell me to slow down. Telling a person who stutters to slow down is embarrassing and demoralizing; particularly when it's in front of a group of people. For some reason, it hurt more when family would say it than when friends would say it.

CHAPTER 4

Basketball

I initially played on a football team when I was ten years old. Although I was a pretty good wide receiver and defensive end, I quickly realized football was not for me. I had a stuttering experience in football that turned me away quickly. On the offensive side of football, particularly in little league, our offensive plays were given by the coach from the sideline.

I played pretty much every snap (offensive play) but I had times where my coach would substitute me out of the game so I could rest. When he would put me back in the game, or when any offensive players substituted into the game, the coach would give us the offensive play for that particular snap, so he didn't have to shout it from the sideline.

As a person who stutters, this was very uncomfortable. I would have to come into the offensive huddle and shout the play for the quarterback and the entire team to hear. This made me nervous because I was rushed. In between snaps, there was a limited amount of time provided before you would forfeit the snap and lose yardage. On multiple occasions, I would come into the huddle and stutter while saying the play. "RRRRRRIIIIIIIght, FFFFLLLLAAAANNK-KKKK DDDDDEEEEEEPPPPP FFFFFFOURRTTYYYY TTTTTTWO." I didn't like that feeling or the way my team-mates looked at me. They rarely teased me about it, but occasionally they would say, "Come on man," as I was attempting to say the play. They were obviously frustrated with me.

I always played basketball for fun, but at eleven years old, I really dove headfirst into it and played for the eleven and under basketball team at the Brookland Manor Boys and Girls Club. This is where I found my love for basketball. Little did I know, basketball would take me to places I never imagined I would go.

For example, I played in the United States Youth Games tournament in 1999, representing Washington DC's fourteen and under boys' basketball team that competed against other US cities in St. Croix, Virgin Islands, and the entire trip was free for me and my teammates.

In the 9th grade, it was evident I was becoming pretty good at basketball. In the neighborhood, I was given the nick-name "Tony Kukoc" after a well-known National Basketball Association player. He was tall, left-handed, and played the small forward position for the Chicago Bulls.

I, too, was left-handed and played the small forward position and exhibited some of the same basketball skills as Tony Kukoc. I played on several little league Brookland Manor Boys and Girls Club basketball teams and Amateur Athletic Union teams with a guy who would become my best friend, hereafter known as "T3". I consider him to be one of the best basketball players to ever come out of Washington, DC.

Although we were teammates on various little league Brookland Manor Boys and Girls Club teams, we became very close when we were both enrolled at Alice Deal Junior High School in Northwest Washington, DC. He was in the 8th grade, and I was in the 9th grade at the time.

We would catch the Metro Red Line train from the Rhode Island Ave. Metro station in Northeast DC, all the way to the Tenleytown-American University Metro station in Northwest DC, (ten long train stops in between the two stations) and then we walked a half mile to school every day. We were pretty much late for school every day, but this is where we forged a bond. T3's mom had passed away a few years prior, and he was still processing his grief and mourning her death.

We didn't realize the impact we were having on each other at that age by just being there for each other. The brotherhood we shared served a two-fold purpose. It was helping me with my stuttering struggle, and it was helping him work through mourning the death of his mother.

I had what I would perceive as at least a couple hundred or maybe a thousand bad stuttering episodes during my childhood, and T3 probably witnessed at least half of them and never laughed, not one time. Understand, as a child you are super immature and it's so easy to laugh at someone stuttering. I don't know how he didn't laugh along with everyone else, but he didn't, and I thank him for that. During a time when it was hard, I was free to be myself around him, and that truly helped me more than he will ever know.

In DC, junior high school went all the way to 9th grade, even though High School also accepted 9th graders. Entering high school in the 10th grade, I wanted to attend Dunbar Senior High school. Dunbar had just won the DC basketball championship the year before, and the head coach was mutually interested in me playing for his team.

There was not a requirement to complete junior high school before enrolling into High School as a 9th grader, so T3 also enrolled into Dunbar to play on the varsity basketball team along with me, he was that great of a basketball player that the coach wanted him as a freshman on varsity.

As a 10th grader playing varsity, I knew I would not play a lot, but in games that we were expected to win by a lot of points, my coach would put me in the game. I remember one game in particular was coming up against School Without Walls, and it was expected that we would beat them pretty badly, and I would play a lot. A few days before, I didn't feel well, so I missed practice.

The protocol was, if you could not attend practice, you had to call the coach's office phone number, leave a voice message, and you would be excused. But one thing about a person who stutters is we hate leaving voicemails. They intimidated me, so I decided to not call my coach and took a chance on missing practice, and hoped he would just let me play.

The day I missed practice, my mom asked me why I wasn't at practice. Instead of being honest and vulnerable about being ill and my fear of leaving a voicemail, I said, "We didn't have practice."

Fast forward to game day. My mom was present at the game since she expected me to play. The game started, and we pulled to an early lead. As each quarter went by, I was still sitting on the bench. The game ended with me not playing at all.

My coach saw my mom's disappointment and confusion and walked up to her and said, "DaVon missed practice. He knows the rules and didn't follow them. That's why he didn't play."

I was heartbroken. Here I had another opportunity to tell my mom what was really going on with me and my struggles with my stutter, but I froze once again. I hated that I stuttered; I was so disgusted. I didn't know how to talk about it, because still at this point in high school, I had not accepted my stutter.

I went on to play two more years of varsity basketball at Dunbar and became the 2002 DC public high school basketball all-star game Most Valuable Player.

I was also a 2002 McDonald's All-American nominee, which meant I was one of the top 1,100 12th grade boys' basketball players in the United States. I knew I would not be selected to play in the McDonald's All-American game, which aired live on ESPN, and included the likes of Carmelo Anthony, Amare Stoudemire, JJ Redick, and Chris Bosh.

I don't know exactly where McDonald's had me ranked but I can guarantee it was closer to 1,100. I was not highly recruited coming out of High School and although I received interest from college coaches, I never received a basketball scholarship. I went on to earn a partial basketball scholarship as a walk-on freshman at Livingstone College in Salisbury, NC and played one year of Division II collegiate basketball.

CHAPTER 5

College Public Speaking Course

I attended Livingstone College in Salisbury, NC, from 2002 to 2006. Coming from Washington, DC, a fast-paced city, to attending college in Salisbury, NC, a very small, historic and slow-paced city, was a culture shock.

Livingstone College is a private, historically black, Christian college, and is affiliated with the African Methodist Episcopal Zion Church. During my tenure at Livingstone, we had an enrollment of 1,000 students, which is smaller than a lot of high schools.

As a business administration major, I was required to take a public speaking course during my sophomore year. Being a person who stutters, I was extremely nervous.

According to 2020 estimates by Cross River Therapy, "around 15 million people in the world deal with glossophobia (fear of public speaking) on a daily basis, and around 75%

of the world's population (200 million people) feel nervous while speaking publicly to a certain degree."[5]

My course outline included two public speaking assignments. The first assignment had to be at least three minutes, and would take place in the classroom in front of my peers. The other speaking assignment had to be no less than five minutes and would take place in front of the same peers, but in an auditorium, on a stage, and using a microphone. My anxiety was through the roof, and I asked myself, "What if I stutter in front of the class? I will be so embarrassed."

Throughout my childhood, I never attended speech therapy, but I studied my speech pattern and identified certain sounds or words that I could not enunciate without stuttering so I learned what is called covert stuttering. I didn't realize I was doing it at the time but later learned I had been employing that behavior to disguise my condition. The Minnesota State University defines covert stuttering as "those who seemingly speak normally at times, but put loads of pressure on themselves to conceal their occasional bouts of stuttering by using various techniques. These are people who appear to look normal and will also be able to pass off for a non-stutterer for a few times, but ultimately as they say,

---

5   https://www.crossrivertherapy.com/public-speaking-statistics#sources

'One cannot fool everybody all the time.' (Karthik Ranga-nathan)"[6]

Even though I was now a college student, I still hadn't accepted my stutter. I wanted to be fluent so badly.

The day finally came for me to do my first speaking assignment. I wrote the speech to my advantage and only used words I knew I could enunciate without stuttering. I got through the speech without stuttering and thought I did well.

My professor didn't share my opinion. When critiquing my speech, he said, "You talked extremely fast and didn't have any eye contact and didn't look up during your speech."

I agreed. My head was down, looking at my index cards the entire time. I just wanted to get through it without stuttering. As far as I was concerned, that was a win for me.

Preparation for my second speech took my anxiety to another level. The thought of having to stand on a stage and use a microphone was so intimidating. I attempted to use the same method as I previously did; writing the speech to my advantage and practicing it thoroughly. I only used words I could enunciate. Although nervous, I believed my

---

6   https://ahn.mnsu.edu/services-and-centers/center-for-communication-sciences-and-disorders/services/stuttering/information-about-stuttering/serious-information/types-of-fluency-disorders/covert-stuttering/covert-stuttering-ive-got-a-secret--and-its-scaring-me-to-death/

covert stuttering would once again prevail. The day of the second speech was here, and I was up next.

I walked onto the stage and began my speech. My heart was racing as I looked out at the audience. I tried to do better this time at keeping my head up, and I figured I should find an object to look at, straight ahead instead of one of my peers. I was halfway through and thought, "You are almost there." Then I came to a couple of words I thought I wouldn't stutter on. Much to my dismay, it happened—within seconds of each other, "CCCCCCCCCCCCCCCCCCCompany" "OOOOOOOOOOOOOOOOrganization""STTTTRRUCCC-TUREEEERRR"

Everyone laughed, and the professor had to quiet them down.

I was crushed. I practiced so hard and long on this speech to not stutter. I asked myself, "How did this happen? I'm not supposed to stutter on these words." At this time, I preferred to be a covert stutterer. I didn't know how to stutter openly. It just wasn't natural for me. I never felt comfortable enough to stutter shamelessly. At nineteen years old, I had been covert my entire life. I hated stuttering with passion and sometimes directed that hatred toward myself.

CHAPTER 6

The Internship

As I was finishing up my junior year in college, my mom received an email that a government agency, hereafter known as Agency 1, was hiring a large contingent of student interns for the summer of 2005. I applied and got an interview. This was my first real job interview, and I was extremely nervous.

I had summer jobs as a teenager, mainly through the Marion Barry Summer Youth Employment Program in DC, but you didn't have to interview; you applied and were placed at a worksite nearest to your residence. When I arrived for the interview, the two interviewers were welcoming. It was a very relaxed atmosphere, and that put me at ease. I did pretty well in the interview and was offered a job.

Before I was given a start date with Agency 1, I had to obtain an interim security clearance consisting of a background investigation, including a criminal history check. A few months prior, I was cited for reckless driving. I didn't think this would interfere with my security clearance because I had a scheduled court date to settle this issue by paying a fine.

The background investigator called me and stated, "Due to your upcoming court appearance, we have put your interim security clearance on hold." This broke my heart, because the next day, the person who interviewed me called and said, "Sorry to inform you, but we have to move on and select another intern."

I got my court date, attended the hearing, paid the fine, and quickly notified the background investigator so they could grant my interim security clearance. My clearance was granted, but Agency 1 had already moved on without me.

A couple weeks later, as the summer was nearing, I got a call from another person at Agency 1, whom I had never met, and they advised, "Another intern position was created, and if you want it, you got it." I quickly accepted. Although I was in college at the time, I was already a father to a one-year-old daughter, and was about to become a father for a second time to another daughter.

The morning I was set to start my internship, the mother of my kids called and said, "I'm going into labor." Now mind you, I hardly got this internship because of my reckless driving citation and interim security clearance issue. Secondly, they offered the job to me one week prior and said to show up on this date and time.

Who do I call? I didn't know who, much less have the contact information for my supervisor. At that moment, I panicked. I wanted to see the birth of my second daughter, but I didn't want to mess up this "good ole government job," as some would call it. I was also already self-conscious as a person who stutters and now as a twenty-year-old young adult, with two young daughters. I didn't know how Agency 1 would view me.

I called my mom, and as always, she was there to pick up the pieces.

"Go to work," she said. "I will go to the hospital and keep you posted."

So, I opted to go to work. On my first day, I was there the entire day. Throughout the orientation, I kept checking my phone for updates. Luckily, since it was the first day, they dismissed us early. I got on the Metro and rushed to the hospital. Fortunately, my baby girl had not come into the world just yet. No more than an hour after I arrived, she was delivered, and I was there to witness it. I truly believe she waited for me to get there.

During my summer internship at Agency 1, I met a young lady who I soon found out stuttered as well. We sat next to each other at an intern luncheon, and as I started talking …

"Do you stutter?" She asked.

"Yes."

"So do I." She had the biggest smile on her face.

I was so happy. I was twenty years old, and it was the first time I met someone my age who stuttered.

For so many years going through school, I always thought I was the only person who stuttered because I never met anyone who stuttered at school. We connected a couple times for lunch during the summer, but after the summer ended, we returned to our respective colleges and lost contact.

My summer internship was a success. I had the opportunity to work on some projects which led to one individual giving me a heads-up about two potential full-time positions that would become available within the next year. I sent an email to the person who was hiring, introduced myself, told him I would graduate in a year, and would love to be considered for one of the open positions.

Even though I only saw this guy in passing and never had any conversations with him, he told me the job was mine, and he would begin the process of converting me from an intern to a full-time government employee effective after my college graduation. Only God could have made that possible. I was so grateful and appreciative. As a young father of two daughters, heading into my senior year of college and already having a job lined up, really helped me focus on finishing up my last year of college strong.

CHAPTER 7

First Full-Time Federal Government Job

I officially began my full-time federal government career at Agency 1 in the summer of 2006. I was assigned to the Hotline branch as a Hotline Investigator. We were responsible for the receipt, processing, and referral of complaints related to waste, fraud, abuse, and criminal misconduct regarding Agency 1 programs, personnel, and funds. I was so excited but also nervous.

During my first couple of months, I felt as though I was not doing well. My work would get returned to me with errors pretty frequently, and it was hard to get a read on whether my boss really liked me. He didn't talk to me much, but over time, I learned that was just his personality. He was not warm and fuzzy with anyone.

I learned early on that it was important to not just make the corrections when I made errors, but actually look at the errors, study them, and try to understand what I was doing wrong, so I wouldn't continue to make the same errors. Six months into my job, my boss acknowledged my accomplishment of reducing my error rate and I was ecstatic.

Throughout my childhood, I never stuttered while saying my name when meeting people or introducing myself, but when I started my federal government career, I really struggled with the "day" sound of my name. I started to stutter my name regularly. It was quite shocking to me that I would stutter my name at this stage of my life; especially since I had never done it before.

Although my name is spelled Da-Von, it is pronounced Day-von. Over the years, people would call me Duh-Von, with the "Duh sound instead of the "Day" sound as intended. I would correct them, but after a while, I got tired of correcting people and would answer to Duh-Von.

More often than not, after being introduced to new people at Agency 1, I would shake their hand and try to move directly into the conversation to avoid stuttering while saying my name. Once again, I exhibited another covert stuttering behavior—avoidance.

I soon realized that if I introduced myself as Duh-Von, I wouldn't stutter. Consequently, I adopted the Duh-Von pronunciation at work, especially since everyone already called me that. I kept the Day-von pronunciation for my personal life.

One of the many duties of my initial government job was returning voicemails from callers who wished to file a complaint. Agency 1 did not have a 1-800 Hotline number for individuals to call and speak to a live Hotline investigator. However, they provided a phone number on their website for callers to use to leave voicemails to report a misconduct issue. Here we go again with the voicemails. The challenge with returning voicemails was the people I was trying to reach were not always available when I returned their call. Our policy was to call the person back a maximum of three times. If they didn't answer on the third attempt, we were required to leave a voicemail with instructions. When it was my turn to call someone back, I would pray to God every time that they answered by the third call.

Something about the voicemails scared me to death. I always preferred to talk to a person. I felt more comfortable with that type of interaction. In my mind, that "please leave a message after the beep" invitation was scary. Again, I think it was the fear of stuttering and that people would have a recording of me stuttering in the voicemail versus just a memory if I stuttered while talking to them on the phone.

After my first two years at Agency 1, my boss retired, and they restructured my branch and I reported to a new Hotline Director. This new Hotline Director had a different leadership style. He invested in mentorship and profession-al development. He encouraged all the staff to take profes-sional developmental training courses designed to enhance our career knowledge, skills, and competencies. While these courses were voluntary, I understood their value early in my career and took several courses.

I may not have been the most talented, best educated, or the smartest person in any given room, however, I made it a point to leverage my key strength to always be the hardest working person in the room. I learned as a basketball player that doing the things others didn't want to do—diving for a loose ball, taking a charge, sprinting back on defense, attempt-ing to block shots, and being willing to make hustle plays—those are the most impactful plays in a basketball game. The best scorer is the most notable player on the basketball court, but the "Hustle Guy" is the most impactful.

Heading into my third year, my boss hired four new em-ployees, and I became their mentor/team leader. I was tasked with training a new crop of government employees and pro-viding mentorship. This was exciting for me because I knew my job pretty well at this point. Except for one or two people, prior to these new younger employees arriving, I primarily worked with more seasoned employees and always felt out of place. I could not relate to them, and they could not relate to me. Enter some youth, and I was excited. I quickly formed a co-worker turned friendship with the new staff and we even went out to happy hours together.

By the time I reached my fourth year at Agency 1, people recognized my potential and leadership skills. I received excellent annual performance ratings and performance-based cash awards, but I thought everyone got those. One of my superiors told me, "One day you will be running the Hotline Branch." I didn't believe him. I thought he was just being nice.

In addition to my leadership skills, another superior recognized the way the newer employees gravitated toward me. She said, "You have great leadership potential. I see how the newer employees listen to you, and follow your lead. One of the keys to effective leadership is the ability to influence people and have them rally behind you, and the mission of the organization."

Another superior called me the "Czar" of my particular field. That was a tremendous honor, but again, I thought all these people were just being nice to me.

Another superior said, "One day you will be a Senior Executive" and that's when I really told myself, "These people are full of crap. I stutter. I will not be any of those things nor will I accomplish anything they are saying."

I certainly didn't believe in myself. I thought I was pretty good at my job, but leading a whole branch or division? How was that even possible? I stutter! No one would take me seriously. Little did I know, these people saw something in me I didn't see in myself at the time.

At Agency 1, my position was considered a starter position. People usually worked in the Hotline for a couple years, then transitioned to become a Criminal Investigator (Special Agent). My position as a Hotline Investigator was more on the investigative support side. While investigative support staff are essential, they are not as important as the Special Agents. Special Agents had better benefits, pay, and early retirement. Although highly desirable, the thought of me as a Special Agent just didn't make sense. As a person who stutters, I didn't think I could do it.

When opportunities to pursue a career as a Special Agent arose, I made excuse after excuse. I thought, "Who will take me seriously? Imagine me in an interview room sitting across from a criminal, attempting to ask questions and interrogating them while stuttering. The criminal would not take me seriously and they would use that against me."

I was also afraid to fail the three-month Special Agent Training Course; not because I didn't think I was smart or skilled enough, but it all hinged on my fear of stuttering, the rigorous interview and interrogation training, and the court testifying training that I thought I would fail because of my stuttering.

Heading into year six at Agency 1, my career was flourishing. Even though I lacked self-confidence, had very low self-esteem, and the negative self-talk would not be silenced, I looked and acted like a confident person. However, underneath that persona, I was far from it.

One security guard that worked at Agency 1 said, "I'm going to call you The Cool Breeze." When I asked him to explain, he said, "It's just how you walk so confidently every day. You are cool, man." I looked at him, and thought to myself, "I wish. If only he knew. Not only was I struggling internally, I was a fraud, an imposter." It was all I knew how to do. I never wanted to show weakness.

CHAPTER 8

The Nervous Guy

had reached the highest level I could achieve at Agency 1 as a Hotline Investigator, and accomplished some incredible things in my six years there. With no room for advancement at Agency 1, I started searching for a new job in the spring of 2012 with other federal government agencies that had promotion potential within their Hotline Divisions.

After applying with another federal agency, hereafter known as Agency 2, I was called for an interview.

I was extremely nervous the day of my interview. Although this was only my second interview, it was really my first official job interview competing against people for a position, and I did not know what to expect. The last interview I had was nearly seven years prior, and it was for an internship.

Now, I was competing with other government employees for a position as a Hotline Investigator for Agency 2. I took the Metro to my interview. It was April 2012, and on this day, it was an unusual ninety degrees in the spring season. My interview was at 3:00 p.m., which was around the time the temperature usually hit its peak. I did not realize the office where I was interviewing was nearly five long blocks away from the Metro station. I was nicely dressed in a suit, and as I started to walk, I began to sweat profusely; I mean a lot. I arrived at the entrance of the building where the interview was taking place, and it looked like someone splashed my face with water; that's how bad I was sweating.

The receptionist let me in, and I immediately asked to use the bathroom so I could dry off. Unfortunately, I underestimated how long it would take me to get to the interview, so I was only there five minutes early. Consequently, I didn't have time to dry off fully. The receptionist walked me into the interview room, where four people sat at the interview table. Two additional people were in the corners of the room.

My heart dropped. "Why are there so many people in this room? What type of interview is this?" The interview started, and they asked me a series of questions. I was literally having an out-of-body experience again. My covert stutter techniques had gone out the window. I can honestly look back and say I was not prepared for the interview questions or the amount of people in the room.

I stuttered with every response and wanted to run out of the room once the interview ended. I left the room thinking,

"These people are laughing at me. They probably think I'm illiterate." In reality, I am a person who stutters, and when combined with a lot of anxiety, the results are not exactly stellar.

Although I applied for several jobs in the spring of 2012, Agency 2 is the only call I received for an interview. I was convinced I blew that interview. A couple months had gone by and in July 2012, Agency 2 called me asking if I was still interested in the Hotline Investigator position I had previously interviewed for. And if so, it was available, and if I accepted, it was mine.

I was so confused; my recollection of the interview was that it had gone horribly. But I had an offer on the table, so I put that behind me and accepted the position. I was set to start in September 2012.

My first week on the job was primarily meeting people, orientation, and the start of my initial training. I was scheduled to meet with a director of another division as part of my orientation and one-on-one meet and greet schedule.

This particular director was an African American male, who was a lot older than me. Once the meeting started, and it was going well, he told me what his division does and the correlation with his division and the Hotline Division I worked for. He then proceeded to tell me he was at my interview. Now remember, there were six people in the room. He was not one of the four interviewers, but was one of the two spectators in the corners of the interview room.

I did not remember seeing him, but I said "Ok."

He finished his statement by saying, "I heard you fumbling over your words and stuttering a lot in your interview. You were really nervous. I recommend you go to public speaking classes, so you can become comfortable. I know that helped me."

I was stunned, literally speechless. I still believed in my heart that my stutter was a secret, and that I was the best covert stutterer, and that no one knew I stuttered; even after I acknowledged to myself that I stuttered in the interview. Also, why would he say that to a person who stutters?

I believe he was coming from a good place; he did not know I was a person who stuttered. He just thought I was this nervous guy. I regretted not speaking up and advocating for myself and my stutter, not as an excuse, but as the truth. I should have told him "That's how I talk sir, I have stuttered my entire life," but again, acknowledging my stutter was not natural for me. I still had goals of one day becoming fluent and I still had not accepted my stutter. For the most of my life, I refused to even utter the word "stutter."

Having spent six years at Agency 1 working in the Hotline Division, I came to Agency 2 with a wealth of Hotline knowledge. I quickly moved through my training faster than anyone expected, and I was released to work independently.

Much like Agency 1, part of my Hotline duties at Agency 2 was returning Hotline voice messages, because Agency 2 did not have a 1-800 Hotline number for individuals to call and speak with a live Hotline Investigator to report misconduct.

Agency 2 gave me my own office, and for some reason that gave me a level of comfort knowing that I was no longer in a cubicle and no one could hear me returning a call. I was promoted to a Lead Hotline Investigator and given additional team leader responsibilities. I really enjoyed training and leading others, and it gave me satisfaction. A lot of the times, it helped me escape my fears of stuttering. I figured my knowledge and work ethic would overshadow my stutter, causing people to focus less on my stutter, and more on my skills and what I bought to the organization.

CHAPTER 9

The Wife

I met my wife in the summer of 2010, when our siblings introduced us to each other. We started dating in January 2011. Dating as a person who stutters was intimidating, especially for me as a covert stutterer. I was so nervous and worried that she would look at me crazy the first time I stuttered. I went to pick her up for the first date and we went to a restaurant at the National Harbor in Maryland.

I was being my typical self, very covert, doing my hide-my-stutter dance when she asked me, "What high school did you go to?"

Although my name starts with a "D" sound, certain words that start with the letter D, gave me trouble and I would stutter when I pronounced them. I knew saying "Dunbar" without stuttering was going to be hard, but I went for it. Trying to be covert while answering the question caused my voice to raise. I don't know why, but I replied very loudly,

"DDDDDDDDDDunbar." Wow! The stutter was only half the problem this time. It was how loud I said it while stuttering that startled people at neighboring tables. How embarrassing, but I didn't let that silence me for the rest of the date. We continued on and had a great time.

My wife was really involved in church when we started dating. She regularly attended Sunday service, sung in the young adult choir, and was a member of the praise and worship team at her church in Temple Hills, MD. I was raised and baptized in the church as a child, but at the time, I didn't have what I considered a strong relationship with God because I drifted away from the church.

The church is not a requirement for someone to have a connection with God, but I have always believed corporate worship was essential and that the church gives us guidance on how to follow God; helping us stay consistent in our worship and spirituality.

At least once every couple of months while dating, my wife would invite me to church, and I would respectfully decline. During our first year of dating, I went to her church one time when she was involved in a musical production.

After our first year of dating, her request came more frequently. Her desire was for someone she was dating, who claimed they were a Christian and believed in God, to go to church, not for her, but to strengthen his own relationship with God. I had always admired that about her.

She even stated, "If my church is not the church for you, I will accompany you to other churches, and would consider joining another church with you, if that's your desire."

I was like many people. I had a desire to join a church, but I didn't think I was ready, because I didn't believe I was living a holy life. I thought I had to have it all figured out first. In all actuality, the church is a place to come when you are broken and in need of fixing … in other words, "Getting right with God."

I proposed to my wife in September 2012 and joined her church that same month. We quickly planned our wedding for September 2013. Typically, for adults who stutter, our family, friends, partners, and spouses take our lead regarding an actual conversation about our stuttering. While dating my wife, I never bought it up, and she never bought it up either. It was a part of me, and she accepted it.

Stuttering never became an issue with communication while dating or when a sore subject came up. During the wedding planning, as the time got closer, specifically within three months of the wedding day, I became extremely concerned and nervous about the wedding ceremony. Part of the pre-marital process required us to have three pre-marital counseling sessions with our pastor, who would be the officiant for our wedding.

During the first session, the pastor opened up with a word of prayer and closed with a word of prayer. The second session, he opened with a word of prayer and at the conclusion of the session, he asked me, "DaVon, are you comfortable closing us out in prayer?"

I paused and said, "Sure." But I was nervous and overwhelmed with fear. I have prayed before, but typically it had been when I was alone. I viewed it as an intimate conversation between me and God. I was intimidated, and thought, "What if my prayer isn't good enough? I'm standing here with a pastor who specializes in prayer. He can do this in his sleep." At this point, I had never heard my wife pray out loud, but I knew she would be good at praying in front of people. She just seemed wired that way.

I wasn't prepared to pray. The optimum word being "prepared." Part of my covert stuttering technique was based highly upon preparation. I typically stuttered more when I was not prepared for a question or assignment. These circumstances are where covert stuttering was not effective. So, I started to pray "DDDDDDDDDear HHHHHHHeavenlllllllly Faaaaaattherrrr IIIIIIIII CCCCCCCCCommmmmmeee, Tooooooooo, Youuuuuuuu, TOOOODADADADADAY. TTTTTTHANKKKKKNNNING Youuuuuuuuuuu ..." I stuttered through the entire prayer.

This was the first time my wife had ever heard or seen me stuttering that much at one time. I had become so proficient at covert stuttering that she and others considered my stuttering mild and not very often. I was so embarrassed.

As we walked to the car after this pre-martial session, my wife said, "I never heard you stutter that much at one time."

"Yeah, I was nervous." There was no doubt I was nervous, but one thing she didn't know was that I would stutter even more if I wasn't so ashamed of my stutter. I was still trying to do everything in my power to be fluent, and it was very exhausting and taxing on my mind and body.

A couple months before our wedding, my wife and I were invited to a lounge in DC to celebrate her friend's birthday. We were engaged at this point, and I had met a lot of her friends. At this event, there were other people there that I had not met.

As I previously stated, as an adult, it became increasingly difficult to say my name without stuttering. Introductions were a huge challenge and obstacle, but they were inevitable.

At the lounge, people were introducing themselves. A guy approached me that my wife didn't know, but he was part of the group we were hanging out with.

He said his name, which I do not remember, but I vividly remember attempting to say my name. It came out as "DDDDDDDDaaaVon."

The man laughed. "This guy must be drunk already."

My wife was standing beside me. She paid the comment no mind, smiled, and continued talking to one of her friends. My reaction wasn't so nonchalant; I was totally embarrassed. As a person who stutters, I always feared embarrassing someone I was dating or married to.

I never wanted them to feel ashamed of being with me. It was a huge insecurity of mine. My wife handled the situation as she should have. I laughed the comment off and tried to enjoy the night, but in all honesty, I felt horrible and embarrassed. I could have easily told the guy, "No, I'm not drunk, I stutter."

I was definitely not drunk, but to me that would have been as embarrassing as the act of stuttering on my name. I had no love for my stutter. At twenty-eight years old, I still hated that I stuttered. I still hated myself because of my stutter. The question, "Why Me?" always ran through my mind. Regrettably, I even questioned God on multiple occasions throughout my life.

After the incident at the lounge, I decided I needed to have an actual conversation with my wife about my feelings toward stuttering. We had been together for over two years, and it was the first time I bought up stuttering to my wife.

Confidently, I told her I was not nervous about marrying her, and then I shared my deepest fear. I was actually nervous about stuttering in front of 200 people on our wedding day, which was most important to us.

She comforted me and said, "Don't worry about that. You hardly stutter. You will do fine. It's going to be a wonderful day."

What was important in her response was the comment, "you hardly stutter." What she didn't know was being a covert stutterer had become a full-time job. Now around her I could let some good "stutters" rip, but for the most part, I was a full-time covert stutterer. It was embedded in me to the point of literally being part of my DNA.

The wedding day was here, Sunday, September 1, 2013, and we had an early evening wedding. Perfect. I had the entire day to worry about stuttering. I arrived around noon, checked in, and got ready. My groomsmen were scheduled to arrive later in the afternoon.

Having plenty of time, I decided to go to the Friday's restaurant across the street where I sat at the bar, grabbed some food, and had one alcoholic beverage that was disgusting; I didn't finish it. I called one of my brothers, who was my best man, and asked, "I know you are not supposed to come for another hour or two, but if you are ready, come now. I'm by myself and I'm freaking out."

He came and reminded me about my uncle who got married a few years earlier and how we took a couple of shots of alcohol to relax. Then he suggested we take a couple shots of alcohol to take the edge off. When the rest of the groomsmen came, that's what we did, and it definitely took the edge off. The limousine arrived, and we were off to the wedding.

I gave myself quite a few pep talks leading up to the wedding. I told myself, "Focus on your bride. You know she will look beautiful, and at the altar it is just you, her, and the pastor. Don't focus on the audience." That is exactly what I did. Once she walked down the aisle, I burst out in tears of joy, telling myself I had no reason to fear. She was gorgeous. I remembered she loved me, and my stuttering. Fueled by determination, I decided if I stuttered at the altar, so be it. The world will go on. We got through our vows, exchanged the rings, I kissed my bride, and we were off to the reception to celebrate with family and friends and what a time we had.

CHAPTER 10

Start at Agency 3/Son in NICU

I was scheduled to start a new journey at Agency 3 as a Hotline Investigator in the beginning of April 2016. I was looking for a new opportunity and career advancement that Agency 2 couldn't provide. At this time, my wife was pregnant with our son and first child together, hereafter known as DC2.

My wife was in great health leading up to and during the pregnancy and everything was normal until one night in March 2016, when she wasn't feeling well. I took her to the emergency room late that night. The nurses were concerned with her blood pressure levels, especially as a pregnant woman. They ran some tests and determined she was suffering from a condition known as preeclampsia, which is a hypertensive disorder that occurs only during pregnancy.

This condition is most often characterized by a rapid rise in blood pressure that can lead to seizure, stroke, multiple organ failures, and even death of the mother and/or baby. They also determined that she was suffering from hemolysis elevated liver enzymes and low platelets syndrome (HELLP). She was in a very critical situation at this point and the emergency room doctor told us they were not equipped to handle this type of critical situation and immediately expedited her transfer to Georgetown University Hospital in DC. My wife and I were confused and extremely concerned. The ambulance took us to the Georgetown University Hospital, and we checked in. It was now 5:00 a.m. the next morning.

The doctor on staff came in and said to my wife, "Mom, you are very sick, and this situation is extremely critical and dangerous." While my wife was being told how sick and critical she was, she was surprisingly calm. I, on the other hand, was still in a daze, sleep deprived, and not really sure how to process this situation.

The doctor then proceeded to tell us, "Your baby is two pounds and two ounces and severely premature. He has a 50 percent chance of survival, and if he does live, he may develop cerebral palsy." My wife and I burst out in tears as we reflected on how no more than sixteen hours before hearing this news we were laughing and having fun with family, and now what seemed like the worst news possible had just been given to us.

To make things even worse, my wife was extremely sick and as long as she continued to carry our son, her organs would fail. The doctor came back in and said, "If you don't have this baby today, you will definitely have him tomorrow. We have to get him out of you ASAP, but we want to try to give you two steroid shots, twelve hours apart, as an attempt to expedite your son's lungs development." They gave my wife the first shot in the afternoon, and by this time, her blood pressure was stable, but they were watching her organ functions. It was now 8:00 p.m. and the doctor on staff told us he was leaving for the day, and they thought we were good for the night. They would give my wife the next steroid shot early the following morning.

Shift change for the doctors came at 9:00 p.m., and the new doctor immediately said, "We are inducing labor. You will have this baby within the next hour. I cannot risk your life further just to give you another steroid shot for the baby's lungs. Your organs are failing severely."

They took my wife back, and I sat alone in the waiting room. By this time, our family that was there with us all day had gone home. Like us, they thought my wife wouldn't give birth until the next day. As they rolled my wife back to the delivery room and I sat alone waiting, I thought to myself, "Did I just see my wife for the last time?" I immediately started to pray silently, while our family that had previously left raced back to the hospital and accompanied me in the waiting room.

After some time, the doctor came out and said, "Mom and baby are doing fine. Mom is in the recovery room, and you can see her in an hour. The baby has been taken to the Neonatal Intensive Care Unit (NICU), which is standard for premature babies. You will be able to see him soon." That was the best news I could possibly ask for and I thanked God!

My wife was heavily sedated for several hours after giving birth, but I was so happy to see her. A nurse asked me if I was ready to see my son, and she took me and my mother-law to see him. My son, DC2, was so tiny; he was the size of my hand. He was in an Isolette, also known as an incubator.

I couldn't touch him, but they allowed me to look at him. They told me the first couple of hours were critical to his survival. They were not kidding. I was only in the NICU for three minutes before his monitor beeped. The nurses calmly pushed me out of the way, and popped the top on the Isolette because he had stopped breathing.

My heart stopped for a second. I didn't react, frozen in time. I didn't know what to think, but they immediately revived him, closed the Isolette, and said he was ok. They told me to go be with my wife and come back to check on my son in the morning.

My wife was released from the hospital four days after giving birth to DC2, but the NICU doctors told us DC2 would need to stay in the NICU for at least a couple of months, if not longer. The day my wife was discharged, it was hard for us to leave DC2 knowing that distance would be a barrier to having the luxury of seeing him every day. During my wife's four-day stay at the hospital, we frequently went to see him.

We agreed that we would come visit him a couple days a week, because we lived forty-five minutes away from Georgetown University Hospital and figured it would be difficult to come see DC2 every day. But who were we kidding? We came to visit DC2 every evening after work.

My wife was suffering from what we later recognized as postpartum depression. It was difficult for her during DC2's stay in the NICU. She blamed herself for his premature birth and was struggling with processing everything. I was there for her and took the lead on keeping in contact with the NICU nurses. Although we visited him every evening, I called the NICU twice a day to check on the status of DC2. I didn't care about stuttering at all when I called. I was only concerned about how DC2 was doing.

Two weeks before DC2 was born, I was given my official start date at Agency 3. DC2 was originally scheduled to be born in June 2016, but he was born prematurely in March. My original plan was to start at Agency 3 in April 2016, perform extremely well in my training and take leave and request to telework earlier than the original ninety-day training period requirement to telework. Agency 3 had a very flexible telework schedule that allowed employees to telework up to four days per week, after completing a ninety-day training period.

My first two months at Agency 3 were challenging. DC2 was in the NICU, and I had to report into the office every day to complete my training. I was working in Agency 3's Hotline Division, so I knew the subject matter very well. It's what I had been doing since I started working for the federal government.

It was just … I lacked focus, and still had the concerns of how they would perceive me as a person who stutters. I was still very much a covert stutterer. Between hiding my stutter, and the amount of my energy going toward DC2 and his stay in the NICU, I was exhausted.

I would sit in training and wonder how many bradycardia (BRADY) episodes DC2 had during the day. A BRADY is a medical term used to describe an abnormally low heart rate. It's often associated with apnea, which is a pause in breathing lasting no longer than 15–20 seconds. DC2 would regularly have BRADY episodes during his NICU stay.

I came into Agency 3 with a solid reputation for being a great Hotline Investigator. I had my own interpretation about what my reputation was; he is good at his job, but he stutters. Now, this was based on how I felt about myself at the time. I always thought when people talked about me in the workplace stuttering was mentioned first, but I would later learn it was last, if even spoken at all.

Stuttering didn't define me, but at this point in time, I didn't believe that about myself. I was still self-conscious, lacked self-esteem, and didn't think highly of myself, even though I was very successful in my career. It was an odd feeling to have and was very unfortunate.

I only had quick interactions with the Hotline Director during my first two months, but at the start of my sixth week at Agency 3, halfway through my ninety-day training period, he stopped me in passing and said, "I heard you came highly recommended from Agency 2, and quickly learned our processes and skated through our training program, that's impressive.

"I also heard about your son. Has your supervisor allowed you to telework yet? I think we should take the training wheels off the bike, so to speak. You are doing great."

I responded, "No, she has not. I was told I have to wait the full ninety-day period."

He replied, "That is the policy, but you are ahead of schedule as it relates to training, and I heard your son may be coming home from the hospital soon."

DC2 was nearly seven weeks old and the NICU doctors told us he would only need to stay in the NICU one more week and they would be comfortable with him coming home. I talked to my supervisor at Agency 3, and told her my son would be coming home, and I planned to take three weeks of leave and she told me once I return from leave, I could start to telework. I was so thrilled.

The doctors and nurses at Georgetown University Hospital took great care of DC2 and told us they did not see anything during his eight-week stay in the NICU, that they thought would have long-term effects on his ability to live a normal healthy life. My wife and I rejoiced and shouted, "GOD IS GOOD!"

At the eighth-month mark of my tenure at Agency 3, the Hotline Director announced he would be hiring and/or promoting four employees to GS-14 Senior Hotline Investigator positions. I was currently a GS-13 and hadn't been at Agency 3 very long, so I was apprehensive about applying.

There were at least twenty-five GS-13 employees, including myself, currently employed in the Hotline Division and many of them had been there for over ten years. Rumors around the office claimed the more tenured employees would get promoted to GS-14. But I applied anyway because I had nothing to lose and everything to gain.

I interviewed, and I felt pretty good about how I did in the interview. It was a two-person interview panel, conducted by the Hotline Deputy Directors. I previously had minimal interactions with the deputy directors and really wanted to impress them. At this point in my career, I possessed nearly twelve years of Hotline experience. Now I just needed to show it in the interview. I left the interview feeling pretty good.

I gave myself a "B" grade. I put on my best convert stuttering show during the interview.

After a week or two had gone by, I received an electronic notification that I received one of the Senior Hotline Investigator positions at a grade of GS-14. That was a pretty significant achievement for a thirty-two-year-old.

Federal government pay is based on government-regulated pay scales, and over 70 percent of federal employees are paid according to the General Schedule (GS). The system has fifteen grades, starting at GS-1 and going up to GS-15, and there are ten steps within each grade. At thirty-two, I was one grade away from the top of grade schedule. I had always been a pretty modest guy, but this was a monumental achievement. I called a lot of my family members, specifically those who were familiar with the federal government. They showered me with love and compliments because they knew how significant the accomplishment was.

CHAPTER 11

I'm Sick Boss

I was now a Senior Hotline Investigator, which came with a lot of senior level responsibilities. For example, I was expected to conduct briefings for groups of different sizes and do presentations. I didn't mind small groups; five-to-ten people was manageable, but I was terrified to do a briefing or presentation in front of a large group. My first briefing as a Senior Hotline Investigator was supposed to be to a group of my peers. As team lead for a project, I had to present our plan of action which was very detailed.

I emailed the team, and for informational purposes only, copied the Hotline management team. The briefing was only for the people directly on the team, my peers. It was the day of the briefing, and we were all in the conference room; my peers were there; it was seven of us in the room and one person on a teleconference.

The director and one of the deputy directors walked in. They wanted to sit in on my briefing. I immediately got extremely nervous and started shaking. I was silently asking myself, "Why are they in here? Are they testing my briefing skills? Do they want to make sure I'm giving proper direction?" So many thoughts were running through my head.

The briefing started; I turned my covert stuttering switch on high. I silently told myself, "This is your briefing, own it." I tried to focus on my subject matter and not on who was in the room. I felt comfortable because I had visual aids. I was using PowerPoint to do my briefing, so in my mind, eyes were on the screen and not on me. Once the briefing was over, the Hotline Director walked over to me and said, "That was a great briefing." I was thrilled and felt great.

The next request was for me to do a presentation at a training course because I was considered a subject matter expert in a specific area. This presentation would be in a large conference room, with over forty people in attendance.

Now, as I stated, small groups I could work with, but forty people … I couldn't do it. I figured I would be so nervous my covert stuttering techniques would not work; I was sure of it. I agreed to do the presentation and the night before, I couldn't sleep. I woke up panicking in a cold sweat. I asked myself, "What if you stutter in front of forty people? How could you ever recover?" I literally talked myself out if doing the presentation.

I have an eye condition called blepharitis, which is a common inflammatory eye condition that would randomly cause one or both of my eyes to become crusted, itchy, irritated, and red. I remembered the first time it had happened. I took a picture of my eye and saved it in my phone.

The morning of the presentation, I felt horrible. I didn't sleep well. I was thinking of an excuse. I didn't know what to do, so I sent that picture to my supervisor and called in sick. I asked myself out loud, "What is wrong with you? You applied for this position, got selected and now you are scared? What a coward!"

Well, it doesn't end there. Public speaking was a part of my new job duties. Another assignment came for me to do a briefing for over forty people once again. OH NO! I can't do this! Why do they keep assigning public speaking assignments to me? I don't want to do it. I am scared I will stutter and be embarrassed. Here I am at thirty-two years old, never having openly talked about stuttering in the workplace or shared with a supervisor my fears of public speaking and stuttering.

The day before the briefing, I had already talked myself out of it. Now I was looking for another excuse. I thought what if I go to work and tell them I have a sore throat. They will feel bad for me and get someone else to do the briefing for me. It was a chance I was willing to take because I didn't want to call off of work for two consecutive speaking assignments. It was also a briefing that someone else had done prior to my promotion anyway, so I knew they could find a replacement last minute.

I practiced my sore throat voice, but it wasn't raspy enough. I thought about when I watch sporting events. Sometimes when I'm very loud, screaming makes my throat sore and voice raspy. The issue was my wife and kids were in the house.

I couldn't just randomly scream to make my throat sore. So, I went into the basement of our home, grabbed a pillow, and screamed "Aaaaah, Aaaaah" into the pillow to muffle the sound and did this several times until my throat hurt. Yes, I got it. The only issue was I didn't think through the possibility of my throat not hurting the next morning, and I was right, this plan failed.

I drove to work the next morning, with my throat not hurting, but my mind made up about not doing this briefing. I walked into the office and said in a very low voice, "My throat hurts. I will try to do the briefing this morning and then go home."

My supervisor said, "No, don't worry about it. Thanks for even driving in and willing to try. Go home. Someone else will do it."

It worked. Another successful escape from facing the real demon I was dealing with, which was not the stuttering itself, but my fear of stuttering and how others perceived it.

I was always just a social drinker as an adult. I never drank alcohol in excess and never felt the need to drink to cope with my stutter. I didn't even like the effects of excess drinking that caused hangovers.

Besides my wedding day, where I took a couple shots of alcohol, which was a ritual for some men to relax before their wedding ceremony, alcohol would typically exacerbate my stuttering. I never considered that it would help with my stutter, but I was considering turning to alcohol as a coping mechanism for how I felt about myself. I was suffering mentally and didn't know what to do.

My father battled with substance abuse much of his life, so I kept that in mind when I was thinking of turning to alcohol to cope. Even considering this as a possible solution, I acknowledged I had officially hit rock bottom. It was time for me to get some help. I had become depressed because I felt like a complete coward after having bailed on my responsibilities on two consecutive occurrences at work, because I was scared and I felt bad about it. I was a fraud.

CHAPTER 12

Therapist, Please Help Me

At thirty-three years old, it was clear I had mental health issues. The lengths I was willing to go to avoid public speaking because of my stuttering was definitely a serious problem and I needed help from a professional, so I sought help from a therapist that specialized in mental health.

The Mass General Brigham Maclean Hospital stated "People of all ethnicities and cultures experience mental health conditions, and Black individuals experience mental health challenges at rates similar to other groups.

"However, when considering the mental health of Black Americans, it's important to look at historical and cultural factors, some of which have led to significant disparities. For example, 25% of Black people seek mental health treatment when needed, compared to 40% of white people.

"The stigma of mental health isn't new to the Black community. Martin Luther King Jr. reportedly had severe depression during periods of his life and refused psychiatric treatment, even when urged to seek care by his staff. Unfortunately, that scenario continues to be common today, with African Americans not seeking mental health care because of stigma.

"The root of mental health stigma among Black people can be traced back to slavery. At that time, it was commonly thought enslaved people were not sophisticated enough to develop depression, anxiety, or other mental health disorders.

"Such nuanced descriptions for depression and other mental illnesses—adopted by the Black community and passed on from generation to generation—led to underestimating the effects and impact of mental health conditions. Also, it strengthened beliefs that a psychiatric disorder is a personal weakness."[7]

Pregnant with our second son, my wife was due to give birth in August 2018. My anxiety was pretty high during the second pregnancy since my wife was considered "high risk" because she suffered from preeclampsia and HELLP syndrome during her pregnancy with our first son, DC2. On the other hand, my wife was confident and regularly encouraged and reminded me that "God's got us."

---

7   https://www.mcleanhospital.org/essential/black-mental-health

In the summer of 2018, I made an appointment with a therapist. I told my wife only a piece of the story about what was bothering me; my anxiety was high because of work and the pregnancy. I didn't mention my stuttering. During my first session, the therapist had me complete a survey, then he asked me a couple of questions, and I started to talk. At the end of our first session, he commented that I didn't talk about the stresses of life that typically cause anxiety and stress in adults, such as relationships/marriage, work, kids, and death. He said I put work on my survey but didn't mention it once. I didn't realize it, but he told me I talked a full hour about my stutter, and he said that's your problem right there.

During the next several sessions, we focused on positive thinking, daily affirmations, and the cognitive-behavioral therapy technique of shifting my thinking from negative to positive to help combat the anxiety.

One session he stated, "Ok, I am familiar with the federal government. You are thirty-three years old, you have been a GS-14 for over a year, and you are an African American male that stutters. Even if you don't believe it, people know you stutter and you're still successful. You already won, accept it, and let go. Wake up every morning and say 'I am the man. I won.'"

The therapist was completely right. Fear can be crippling and negative thinking about oneself is a serious issue, but it can change if the work is put in to change it. The therapist also helped me discover I suffered from imposter syndrome.

BetterUp defines imposter syndrome as "The condition of feeling anxious and not experiencing success internally, despite being high-performing in external, objective ways. The condition often results in people feeling like "a fraud" or "a phony" and doubting their abilities.

"With imposter syndrome, a person doesn't feel confident or competent, regardless of what they achieve. They don't experience the joy of success because they are always waiting for their inadequacy and fraudulence to come to light.

"Imposter syndrome can cause people to feel a sense of time running out. It's as if people have been putting on an act and they can't keep the act up much longer. This is despite all evidence to the contrary."[8]

I also discovered that I was self-loathing which is consistent with self-doubt and self-hate talk. Medical New Today states "Having feelings of self-doubt now and then is often not a cause of concern. For some people, though, these feelings and negative thoughts can affect all areas of a person's life, including how they behave and live.

"It can lead to self-punishment, isolation, and even more severe health conditions like depression and anxiety disorder.

---

8   https://www.betterup.com/blog/what-is-imposter-syndrome-and-how-to-avoid-it

Self-loathing is a pattern of thoughts or feelings of self-hatred and extreme criticism of oneself. It involves a negative internal narrative that continuously shames, judges, demeans, and finds fault in the self.

"Each person has an inherent worth and value. Yet a person with self-loathing tends to have a strong, critical inner voice that constantly shames and berates them for every flaw they have or mistake they make. This constant negativity may influence how a person views the world. They may not even be aware of their unhealthy thought patterns. People with self-loathing tend to minimize or ignore the positive and recognize only the negative things in their lives."[9]

I was definitely suffering from imposter syndrome and self-loathing. It was becoming more and more difficult to be a covert stutterer. The work I had to put into hiding my stutter was exhausting and I needed it to stop, immediately. I called myself a "fraud" several times, and literally hated the person I had become. I never felt worthy of my achievements because I stuttered.

I even thought I was only successful and kept getting promoted because people felt bad for me, and that made no sense, but it was a good explanation to help me survive this unhealthy life I was living.

---

9   https://www.medicalnewstoday.com/articles/self-loathing

I continued my therapy sessions for a couple more months and then, after a normal and healthy pregnancy, my wife gave birth to our second son in August 2018. I didn't go back to therapy after my son was born. I felt as though I had the answers and I now needed to put the work in to change my harmful behaviors.

One of the last things my therapist told me was, "You need to get around some people who stutter, find a community. You are not alone. There are many people who stutter and are going through the same challenges as yourself. You need them more than you need me. I will keep taking your money if you want me too, but the stuttering community is who you really need."

I started to do research in November 2018 on stuttering organizations and came across the National Stuttering Association (NSA) website. I remember the day I typed "stuttering organizations." My heart was beating so fast, I didn't understand why I was so nervous, I was only researching. I immediately exited the website after five seconds; I didn't even read anything. I was not ready. I told myself I would try again some other time.

CHAPTER 13

"The Shift"—A Conversation that Changed My Life

In the spring of 2019, Agency 3 created a new branch within the Hotline Division and was hiring a GS-14 supervisor to lead and five additional employees to staff the branch. I knew I was qualified, but I didn't know if it was the right position for me. I was already a non-supervisory GS-14, and it wasn't logical for me to take a lateral position and gain additional responsibilities; not to mention the headaches that came with supervision, with no additional pay.

But I jumped in with both feet. I applied, interviewed, and was offered the position. When I got the job offer, imposter syndrome kicked in—you don't deserve this, you are a fraud. I remembered what I learned in therapy about positive thinking and speaking positively about myself, and heading into this new position, I started to change my perception.

There was a manager at Agency 3, hereafter known as "DR". I was never under his direct supervision, but we did have a rapport. One day, out of the blue, I went into his suite and saw that his office door was open, so I walked in and asked if he had a minute. I didn't have a reason for wanting to talk to him and didn't know why I went into his office. We started to talk. He instantly poured into me and showered me with compliments. The imposter syndrome kicked in. I was thinking, "Here goes someone else lying to me saying how good I am, when in reality I suck. I'm a fraud and a coward."

He told me, "You will be a senior executive one day!"

Without thought or provocation, I confidently said, "Why would anyone ever hire me as a senior executive? I stutter. No one would take me seriously."

DR then responded with passion and vigor, "Let me tell you something, DaVon. Yes, you stutter. We all know, and we don't care."

"You do?" I interrupted.

He continued on without answering my question. "You have been promoted twice since you have been here because you are the very best at what you do. Your stuttering does not define you, it's just one little piece of you.

"I can guarantee you that when someone talks about you in the workplace, the first thing they mention is your infectious personality centered on positivity and your tremendous work ethic. People who work on your team, and those on other teams, are drawn to your ability to lead. You have a unique ability to lead and inspire. It's something that can't be taught. It's built into your DNA.

"People love working with you. This organization is lucky, heck, any organization would be lucky to have you as a future leader. Keep doing what you are doing. Keep the positive attitude and keep putting in the work. Don't give up. There is no limit to what you can achieve, but you have to believe it. I can't believe it for you."

I was in shock. It was almost as if he was angry that I didn't believe in myself. This was the first time, in my thirteen-year federal government career, that I mentioned my stutter. As a matter of fact, it was the first time I even uttered the word "stutter" in the workplace.

DR had nothing to gain by speaking life into me. He didn't have to do that. He saw a young man with so much potential that was broken and didn't believe in himself. DR could have let me beat myself up and felt bad for myself and just responded, "I'm sorry you feel that way" and dropped the conversation.

Instead, he took the initiative and focused on building up my confidence and helped me zero in on my strengths. He didn't diminish my concerns regarding my challenges surrounding my stuttering, but realigned my thoughts and impressions. I was ready to run through a wall after this conversation. I was so pumped up.

I felt free. When I finally said the word "stutter" in the workplace, and actually talked about my insecurities, it no longer held me in bondage. It's funny how the mind works. I thought I didn't stutter at work. I thought I was this super covert stutterer that possessed the power to be fluent all the time at work. I thought no one knew I stuttered at work. I spent so much energy throughout my life trying to be fluent when I never had to. Everyone knew I stuttered, but since it was never discussed, I always felt I was the only one who knew.

That conversation with DR began a seismic shift, not only in my career, but also in my life. I was ready to commit to trying to stutter openly without fear and shame, and DR helped me get to that conclusion.

CHAPTER 14

The National Stuttering Association

It was now December 2019, and I was thirty-five years old. It had been one year since I first started searching for stuttering organizations, which you may recall only lasted five seconds before I quit because I was embarrassed by the thought of needing a stuttering support group.

I resumed the search by visiting the National Stuttering Association (NSA) website and started reading. "The National Stuttering Association is the largest non-profit organization in the world dedicated to bringing hope and empowerment to children and adults who stutter, their families, and professionals, through support, education, advocacy, and research.

"Our annual conference and nationwide network of more than 150 self-help groups for adults, teens, and children who stutter provides unparalleled empowerment, encouragement, and education for people who stutter of all ages.

"The NSA is a trusted resource for explaining the causes, treatment, myths, and facts about stuttering. Our educational materials are used by speech professionals, teachers, employers, families, and medical professionals.

"Over the past two decades, the NSA has taken a leadership role in the advancement of knowledge of stuttering. We proudly support high-quality, innovative stuttering research by offering research funding opportunities, assisting in the recruitment of research participants, and sharing research findings with the stuttering community."[10]

Wanting more understanding, I clicked "Learn More" and NSA's research statement was displayed. "We are advancing both knowledge and understanding of stuttering through our support of research. As the largest stuttering support organization in North America, with access to large numbers of individuals and families affected by stuttering, the NSA® recognizes its unique potential for helping the research community."

The NSA hosts an annual conference with informative workshops, exciting activity, and family fun with people from all walks of life. Connection, engagement, and friendships are formed and strengthened during these events.

As I explored the NSA website and conducted research for the first time in my life about stuttering, which seemed pretty

---

10   https://westutter.org/about-the-nsa/

odd that I never took the time to research something that had bothered me for decades, I was feeling inspired.

I was so inspired and pumped that I decided to record myself talking about having "Faith over Fear." I didn't know what I wanted to say, and I didn't write anything down. I just wanted to get this out. Similar to written journaling, which is an act of writing down personal thoughts, feelings, and insights, this was video journaling.

I was sitting in my car on the morning of December 23, 2019, and I pulled out my phone and pressed the record button. I wanted to speak from the heart. I recorded myself saying, "Nothing is impossible. There are no limits on what you can achieve. I am speaking from personal experiences. I am a person who has had to navigate life with a speech impediment—stuttering. For some reason God keeps blessing me over and over again and I keep defying the odds, so what I want to let everyone know is have faith over fear, because anything is possible."

The video was only twenty-five seconds long, and I believe I watched it over 100 times. I was so proud of myself. That was really the first time I actually said, "I have a speech impediment." It was not natural for me because I never acknowledged or accepted it.

In my mind, the video was a win. I know recording myself talking for twenty-five seconds doesn't seem like a big deal, but for a stutterer, talking openly for twenty-five seconds is no small feat. Although small wins were often overlooked in my life, they were crucial building blocks and steps toward achieving my bigger goals. They always seemed insignificant at first glance, but they played a significant role in building my resilience and character. Small wins are daily achievements and progress toward more extensive accomplishments.

Thanks to my covert stuttering technique, I didn't stutter during this twenty-five second video, but I noticed the tension in my face. Being covert requires a lot of work and on the word "navigate" I didn't stutter, but my lips trembled because I was trying to avoid stuttering. I didn't like how that looked, but again, it was a small win and progress toward my ultimate goals. Another thing I noticed in the video was that I was talking as if there was an audience; as if I had planned to release it.

I thought about it for the next few days, and pondered, "Well, you didn't stutter in the video, so you shouldn't be embarrassed, and the video is only twenty-five seconds. Go ahead and post it to your Instagram and Facebook social media pages."

I have never had a huge following on social media and was never a person who posted much on social media platforms. The couple of times a year I did post something, it was typically family pictures and videos.

On December 29, 2019, I posted the twenty-five second video with the caption *My Quick Story, Faith over Fear* and the video got a couple hundred views on both social media platforms and several comments that included: Great words of encouragement. Keep defying the odds. Amen. This is good, thanks for the reminder. Proud of you. Great testimony. Real talk. Thanks for sharing. Thanks for your transparency, very inspiring. I was shocked at the outpouring of comments and how my little video touched so many people.

I was apprehensive, but went back to the NSA website because I was ready to join a local NSA chapter. The NSA website states "Our network of local chapters are powerful spaces where you can connect directly with your local stuttering community. No matter what point you're at in your stuttering journey, experience the life-changing power of attending a local chapter where you can share your story, bond with fellow people who stutter and allies, and embrace the support of our ever-growing community."[11]

The NSA website had an interactive map that I accessed to find the local chapter closest to my city and state. I lived in Prince George's County, Maryland, which is a suburb of Washington, DC. The state of Maryland had several NSA chapters, but none of them were close enough for me to get to.

---

11   https://westutter.org/chapters/

Therefore, I decided to contact the NSA DC Chapter co-leaders to inquire about joining and getting the meeting details.

One of the chapter co-leaders responded to my message and invited me to their next monthly meeting, which was in January 2020. I had a bunch of mixed emotions; I was excited and nervous, but also still embarrassed. I still looked at this decision to join a chapter as a negative thing. I told my wife about my desire to join a stuttering support group and that it was something I thought would help me on my journey to self-acceptance. She told me, "Go for it, I support you, I think that is great."

It was the day of the meeting, and I was driving to the location of the meeting, and wondered, "What the hell are you doing? Are you going to really go through with this?" I began reminiscing about a couple years prior when I did everything to avoid public speaking at work, even to the determent of my health. I didn't like that feeling and, at that moment, decided I was not going to let fear stop me this time. I parked my car, said a prayer, and walked in.

The room was pretty big, with chairs in a circle. I immediately compared it to a TV version of an Alcoholics Anonymous or Narcotics Anonymous meeting. There were around twelve people, including the chapter co-leaders. At the beginning of the meeting, everyone was asked to introduce themselves and, if they felt comfortable, tell something about themselves.

When it was my turn, I said my name and where I was from and that it was my first meeting. I came into the meeting being my covert self. As people introduced themselves and stuttered, I was amazed. This was only my second time meeting people who stuttered. I had only met a young lady who stuttered while I was an intern at Agency 1. I was thinking to myself, "How do they do that?" It was a mind-blowing experience. The first meeting went well. I didn't talk much, but I engaged in some of the discussion topics. I was just trying to take in that I was actually there.

As I was driving home, I was feeling good about the experience and then imposter syndrome set in; I was really covert in the meeting, so when I spoke up, I didn't stutter. I felt like a fraud; I was in a safe space with people who stuttered, and I refused to let go of my covert stuttering ways and just be free. I thought to myself, "The people in the meeting probably had a group text and said the new guy, DaVon, didn't stutter, not one time. What was he doing here?" Again, this was my own guilt and shame talking. No one at the meeting made me feel this way.

The NSA DC Chapter met monthly, so I had an entire month until the next meeting and I became committed to openly stuttering and tearing down my covert stuttering wall at the next meeting. February arrived and the next meeting was coming up in a few days.

On my way to the next meeting, I gave myself a pep talk and said out loud in my car several times, "I am going to stutter in this meeting, I am going to stutter in this meeting." Now, for people who stuttered, we never gave ourselves pep talks to stutter. If anything, it was the other way around. Baby steps. It would be a small win for me to stutter openly at this meeting. I arrived, parked my car, said a prayer, and walked in. This time, the chairs were not in a circle. They were organized parallel to each other and on the opposite side facing each other. There was a large walkway in the middle.

This meeting started the same as the last, with introductions. The chapter co-leader had some note cards in his hand and stated, "We are about to play a game." He began giving the instructions and asked us to stand at a starting spot, and once he read a question regarding stuttering, we were supposed to take a step if we experienced the scenario he described. The object of the game was to see who took the most steps. This was an excellent ice breaker; I believe I was truly uncomfortable at the first meeting sitting around in a circle.

Once we finished the game, we sat down and dug deeper into some of the topics from the game. At the age of thirty-six, I discovered what covert stuttering was. This is something I had been doing for my entire life and it was refreshing to put a name to the behavior. I took the opportunity in the meeting to talk about my experience growing up and not going to speech therapy and not meeting any other kids who stuttered and feeling alone my entire life dealing with my stuttering.

Then, for the first time in my life, I openly stuttered and felt good about it. I wasn't ashamed or embarrassed. That was a feeling I would never forget. It felt like a huge weight lifted off my shoulders; it was an emotional release I had never experienced in my life, and I loved it.

Calm.com defines emotional pain as "an intense feeling of distress, anguish, or suffering that stem from non-physical sources. Unlike the ache from a stubbed toe or a headache, this type of pain originates from events or circumstances that hurt us deeply on the inside. It could arise from experiences like heartbreak, loss, trauma, or persistent feelings of inadequacy and rejection. While everyone encounters and processes emotional pain differently, its impact on our mental wellbeing is undeniable, making it essential to acknowledge and address it.

"Just like physical pain, emotional pain is a universal human experience. We all feel sadness, anxiety, and anger from time to time. Sometimes, emotional pain can linger subtly in the background. But at other times, it can feel dominant, overshadowing your day-to-day life. Anxiety, for example, can often thread itself into our routines as a constant worry about the future or a lingering fear about our circumstances. People might feel emotional pain for a variety of reasons like navigating challenging relationships, dealing with grief, or struggling with physical illness."[12]

When I left the meeting, I got in my car and cried tears of joy, not sadness. I was happy and overwhelmed with joy. This is what I had been missing my entire life. I couldn't even utter the word "stutter" let alone stutter without having a feeling of disgust because I hated when I stuttered. I wanted more of this feeling; I needed it.

There was a training institute in Washington, DC, that offered leadership development training. I had been a supervisor for nearly a year and decided to register for the New Leader Program, which was a two-week training course, with the first week and second week of the course separated by three weeks. I attended the first week in February and the second week in early March.

I completed the first week, and it was a great experience. The training focused on transformational leadership and team building. The second week focused on leading organizational change and coaching employees. This two-week course was very interactive. We had several individual and group assignments.

I remember one assignment in particular; we were in a small group and the discussion surrounded transparency in the work-

---

12 https://www.calm.com/blog/emotional-pain

place as a supervisor or manager. We were asked to share a challenge we faced and how we overcame it with the small group. It could have been personal or professional, then one person from each small group would share with the larger group. There were thirty-five students in this two-week training course.

Initially, I thought I could share how I navigated becoming a parent at a young age. After much consideration, I decided I should share with the small group my challenges with my stutter.

Even though I had only attended two NSA DC Chapter meetings and was new on my journey of finally accepting my stutter, I threw caution to the wind and went for it. Once I shared with the small group, they all nominated me to share my story with the larger group.

I thought to myself, "See this is what you get for running your mouth. Now you have to say this all over again, but in front of thirty-five people." This was also my first-time public speaking in front of a larger audience since a year or so prior, I was doing everything possible to avoid it. I immediately activated my covert stuttering switch, then at the last minute, I turned it off.

This was my opportunity to stutter openly and freely, while talking about stuttering to a group of people who didn't stutter. I got a standing ovation. Now remember, this is a training course. A standing ovation is not typical for a normal assignment and that was just one of many simple assignments given during this training course. No one, including me, expected my story to have that type of impact. I never imagined that talking about my challenge with stuttering to a group of people who didn't stutter would inspire them.

The important part of this story is: I faced my fear of public speaking in front of a larger audience. I finally released the crippling effect fear had over my mind and broke free of those chains. It was a defining moment for me.

What I didn't realize was, a woman in my class who I didn't interact with during these two weeks also stuttered. With tears in her eyes, she pulled me aside and said, "Thank you for sharing your story. I, too, stutter and had a pretty difficult childhood and challenges navigating adulthood. For you to speak about your stuttering journey with so much confidence; you are an inspiration. I will never forget this moment. I haven't met many people in my life who also stutter."

As I drove home that evening and reflected on the response I received, I was amazed. Stuttering was something I despised for much of my life. I never imagined the words "stutter" and "inspiration" could be used in the same sentence.

It was March 2020, and I was ready for my third NSA meeting. I was excited to share the news with the NSA DC Chapter about my experience with talking about my stuttering journey in my leadership class.

In December 2019, the coronavirus disease (COVID-19) was first identified in an outbreak in Wuhan, China. In January and February 2020, reports of the disease being detected in different parts of the United States started coming in.

The World Health Organization officially declared COVID-19 a Public Health Emergency of International Concern in late January, 2020.[13] The United States Government implemented shutdown orders on March 15, 2020, to prevent the spread of COVID-19. Consequently, the March NSA DC Chapter meeting did not occur as the whole world shut down.

The NSA DC Chapter pivoted to virtual meetings early in the pandemic, but I didn't attend them. I truly missed meeting in person, but just like everyone in the world, my family and I were adjusting to this new normal.

In the fall of 2020, I made a commitment to join an NSA DC Chapter virtual meeting. I missed the connection and in my first meeting back during the introductions, I stated, "I missed these meetings and the connection. Since I joined the NSA DC Chapter in January 2020, my life has changed, and I finally accepted my stutter after all these years."

---

13   https://www.ncbi.nlm.nih.gov/pmc/articles/PMC7253494/#:~: text=In%20late%20January%202020%2C%20WHO,be%20at%20an %20excessive%20hazard.

After I did my introduction, I thought to myself, "Did you just say you accepted your stutter? Do you mean it? Is it real?" I meant every word; it was long overdue. I felt free and finally, without shame, embarrassment, and guilt. Feeling liberated and empowered was a moment I will never forget.

CHAPTER 15

Director Camp

I was flourishing at Agency 3 as a supervisor and in February 2021, I saw a job announcement for a GS-15 Hotline Director position at another federal agency. The Hotline field is small within the federal government. There aren't a lot of opportunities for advancement due to the typical Hotline size and structure, which is small.

During my career, I had to seek advancement by going to other federal agencies. When this opening came up, I was a GS-14 supervisor and as I advanced throughout my career, I never thought I was qualified enough or worthy enough to be a director (manager) of an entire branch or division, particularly a Hotline Division. But at this point, I had accepted my stutter and was not going to let that hold me back any longer.

To reach the GS-15 level in the federal government is a tremendous accomplishment and had always been a long-term goal I set for myself; even though I never thought I would reach it. Less than 3% of the nearly two million federal government employees are GS-15s. The average federal government employee reaches GS-12 or GS-13 by retirement age, and I was fortunate enough to be thirty-six years old and applying for a GS-15 job. According to the statistics, I had not even reached the halfway point of my career.

I completed the application for the GS-15 Hotline Director position at another federal agency, hereafter known as Agency 4. I was selected for a virtual interview to take place in March 2021. We were still in the global pandemic and protocols were still in place in the United States to limit the spread of COVID-19. It was interview day, and I felt confident.

Before the interview, I committed to focusing on my knowledge, skills, abilities, and the core values and principles that got me to this place. I wasn't worried about stuttering; I would be lying if I said it didn't still bother me because it did. By this point, I had come a long way on my journey of accepting my stutter and I was ready to do great in this interview. If I stuttered, it wouldn't bother me.

I also remembered what I had been told two years prior by DR, and I was ready to own the interview.

I took what DR told me into the interview and was outstanding. I exhibited passion and genuineness, which I feel is an undeniable combination, coupled with my knowledge and incredible leadership skills. A week after my interview, I received a call from the selecting official stating, "Hi DaVon, we truly enjoyed your interview last week and want to offer you the position, but we have to conduct reference checks first, are you still interested?"

I immediately replied, "Absolutely," and we ended the call. I thought I did pretty well in the interview, but I figured someone with more life experience and career experience would be offered the job because I was only thirty-six years old. My references were the Hotline Director and two deputy directors at Agency 3.

Within the next week, all three of my references were called, and they all echoed the same sentiments to me after the calls. They were proud of me and assured me I would make a great director.

On the same day my references were called, I had a meeting scheduled with my team and I let them know I had been offered the Hotline Director position at Agency 4.

I felt led to share my feelings about getting the new job. I told them, "I am still shocked I got the job offer. Throughout my life, I have always doubted myself, because I stuttered. I never felt good enough.

"As a kid, I didn't think I would ever be successful, or lead anyone, because stuttering is sometimes associated with a lack of intelligence. That stereotype is based on a lack of knowledge about stuttering by the public. An underlying challenge is fear, which can be crippling if allowed to take root. I no longer operate based on fear, and I do not allow it to consume me anymore."

The team, which I led for two years, told me how much they admired me and enjoyed being a part of my team, but this speech moved some of them to tears. They were so proud of the person I had become. I was becoming more transparent about my challenges with stuttering; I don't know why I was moved to mention that to my team, but I am glad I did. It was refreshing.

In May 2021, I received my start date to become the Hotline Director for Agency 4 and my colleagues from Agency 3 requested to give me a virtual going away celebration. The day arrived for the celebration and I had a ton of emotions. I was excited, nervous, and anxious because I was leaving Agency 3 as a supervisor and going to Agency 4 as a director responsible for an entire operation.

The celebration started, and as I looked at the participation list, I saw that nearly fifty people attended virtually; we only had fifty-five employees in the entire division. I was humbled and honored by the large turnout.

First there was a presentation by my peers which included a slide titled, "What Hotline employees think of DaVon." It contained a list of characteristics my colleagues thought about me. The list boasted a couple hundred words they used to describe me—Amazing, Calm, Charismatic, Dependable, Debonair, Encouraging, Effective, Enthusiastic, Extraordinary, Focused, Genuine, Godly, Humble, Honest, Inspiring, Intelligent, Joyful, Kind, Modest, Organized, Outstanding, Passionate, Responsible, Stupendous, Sophisticated, Trustworthy, Uplifting, and Wonderful—to name some.

At the end of the celebration, they asked me to give a speech. I figured that would be a request, so I had my cell phone out and was ready to record myself as I spoke. I wanted to see and hear myself speak, unedited and from the heart. I wasn't nervous or worried about stuttering. Since my breakthrough at the leadership class, I was making a conscious effort every day to not worrying about stuttering. It was a given. It's what I do, but it's only a small part of me. I am more than my stutter.

My speech was nearly eight minutes long and during part of my speech I stated, "I truly thank you all for your kind words. I appreciate it so much. Over the last few weeks, I have been reflecting on where I have come from, and to start out as a GS-4 intern fifteen years ago, not knowing where I would end up, it's amazing.

"This decision has not been easy. I know some folks have said, 'after all, it's a GS-15.' For me, I can honestly say it's not about the position or the money. You all have said it. For me, it's about the impact. How can I impact an organization, and in the process, how can I inspire? That's what it's all about.

I don't care what grade I'm at, or where I am working; my main goal is to inspire. Folks think success is about how much money you make. It's not. I look at it as, whatever I'm doing, what impact I am having, and is the end result good? It doesn't matter if I'm a GS-5 or an SES.

"Anybody on this call that has spoken with me long enough knows I stutter. It's no secret. I have stuttered my whole life; I was diagnosed at an early age. So, I have always had a chip on my shoulder, and that I had to outwork the next person.

"I wanted my stutter to be the last thing a person mentions about me, and not the first, and I think I have achieved that. Folks always ask me, 'How did you rise from a GS-4 to GS-14 in eleven years?' How? Hard work.

"I challenge anybody on the phone to try to remove fear from your lives. Determine the source of your fear; whether it is work or in your personal life. Once you find the source, put in the effort to eliminate it.

"As soon as I removed the fear, I knew I had the knowledge and skills to do it. Again, overcoming fear is not always easy, and I speak from experience. However, I challenge everybody, whoever is going through anything, to try your best to remove that fear."

After my speech, several people spoke up, some in tears, to thank me for my transparency. I touched so many people with my message that came from the heart, unrehearsed.

One person's response, in particular, comes to mind. This person was new to Hotline, and our interactions were minimal. An email from this person warmed my heart. "Your message was so inspiring. I have a son who stutters. He is in high school and has struggled with his stutter, so to hear you speak so confidently about your stutter, really touched me. You are a true example and inspiration to what my son can achieve if he puts his mind to it."

Another comment came from the Hotline Director. "You turned what you considered a weakness into your greatest strength. People should be honored to work under your leadership. I know I would be."

This part of my speech was two minutes long, and I was feeling so blessed and inspired, so I posted a two-minute video to my Facebook and Instagram accounts. The response was overwhelming. Hundreds of people on both social media sites watched the video, and it had nearly seventy-five comments from people who were proud, inspired, and motivated by what I said in the video.

The day had arrived, nearly fifteen years since I started at Agency 1 as a student intern. I was now the Hotline Director for Agency 4 at thirty-six years old. I was the Inaugural Hotline Director for Agency 4. Since its inception, Agency 4 had a Hotline function, but it did not have an established branch or leader dedicated to the Hotline mission.

Agency 4's Hotline Division lacked an appropriate structure and had inefficient processes that limited their ability to effectively achieve the Hotline mission. I inherited a team of employees, grades GS-5 to GS-14, who were split into two separate intake groups and felt unappreciated and undervalued.

I immediately set a course to change the situation and instill confidence in the team. Focusing on their strengths, I developed their knowledge and skills, was supportive, and most importantly, listened to their concerns. I encouraged positive thinking and attitudes and reinforced their value not only to the team but to Agency 4. I set long-range goals with short-term requirements and implemented effective and efficient Hotline processes. After one year at Agency 4, I received a Distinguished Service Award for Innovation and Outstanding Leadership.

My team was flourishing and bought into the vision and expectations I set for them. One of my team members stated, "It feels good to have a manager who is truly invested in the Hotline mission. We haven't been happy for a long time. We are so glad you are our leader." Another team member said, "You truly have made a difference with this group and continue to make us feel included. Appreciate that."

I took my public speaking skills to the next level at Agency 4 by conducting briefings for groups of differing sizes to include a hybrid audience of nearly 400 people. I also had the opportunity to conduct briefings for international government organizations.

I was invited to be a panelist at a federal government event as a leader in my field. After the event ended, a person in the audience came up to me and said, "I just want to introduce myself and shake your hand. You are a legend in Hotline. I have heard so many great things about you."

I was shocked and honored at the same time as this was a pivotal moment for me. It felt good to be recognized for my achievements and being known as a leader and pioneer in the Hotline community.

To think of the years prior when I ran away from public speaking in the workforce; now I was volunteering, and I was being requested by different organizations because of my stellar briefing skills and subject matter expertise in my particular field. I removed the fear and stopped worrying about stuttering. I knew I was good at what I did, and stuttering was going to happen, so worrying about it any longer was doing more harm than helping.

I also focused on mentorship at Agency 4. Mentorship is monumental to professional development in the workplace, and I became a mentor because I invested in facilitating the personal and professional growth of young government employees and knew the importance of providing guidance, knowledge, and support to future leaders.

Besides being a mentor, I was now a role model for younger government employees because I started at the very bottom as a student intern and ascended to the position of director. I also remembered a conversation I had with the Hotline Director from Agency 3, my former boss, now my counterpart and equivalent. Shortly after I became the Hotline Director at Agency 4, I contacted him and said, "I learned so much about effective leadership by watching you and I always considered you a mentor."

He responded, "Mentoring is a two-way street. I learned just as much from you."

World Educations Services states, "A mentorship is a relationship between two people where the individual with more experience, knowledge, and connections is able to pass along what they have learned to a more junior individual within a certain field. The more senior individual is the mentor, and the more junior individual is the mentee.

"The mentor benefits because they are able to lead the future generation in an area they care about and ensure that best practices are passed along; meanwhile, the mentee benefits because they have proven that they are ready to take the next step in their career and can receive the extra help needed to make that advancement.

"A mentor can help you advance within your field and connect you with opportunities that you might not have otherwise had access to. They do this by sharing their knowledge, helping you identify opportunities in your path, and potentially opening doors for you when the time comes.

"Almost every great achiever in history has claimed that they had a great mentor at some point during their rise to excellence.

"Mentorship is a two-way process. But if it works the way that it is meant to, both the mentor and the mentee will benefit from the experience."[14]

---

14   https://www.wes.org/advisor-blog/definition-of-mentorship/

CHAPTER 16

MTriplel

Time to focus on the positive aspects of my life. I was successful in my career, happily married with children, and I finally accepted my stutter, which was long overdue. Consistent with imposter syndrome, I still struggled with small bouts of self-doubt. Loving your flaws takes a great deal of intention, compassion, and patience. Authentically leaning into our flaws, and doing so with acceptance, is how we can genuinely heal and end the cycle of suffering.

We tend to allow the negative voice to consume us. It rings so much louder than the positive voice, silencing the positive voice at times. I realized I had the power to control the two voices, and I was committed to making the positive voice the dominate one. Forgiving yourself plays a role in self-acceptance, and it's something a lot of us have little experience with. Conditioned to be hard on ourselves, we have trained our minds that forgiveness is for something or someone else, but true forgiveness comes from within.

I also realized it was time to focus on self-love. I had come a long way on my journey of accepting my stutter and now it was time to build upon that and learn to love myself completely and totally. Many times, we love certain things about ourselves, but if we peel back the layers, we discover we don't love ourselves fully. I had spent so much time trying to fix my stutter that it became a huge insecurity within me. I thought that if I could fix it, then everything would be ok. How wrong I was.

I resisted the notion of loving myself for most of my life, worrying that if I loved my stutter, I would never be happy. However, I realized it was really loving my stutter that led to the healing and transformation which created the person I am today. We obsess about certain aspects of our life, but the truth is these things are what they are, and we add meaning and interpretation to them for better or worse.

Verywell Mind states, "Having self-love involves having an appreciation and respect for yourself. That includes taking care of your physical and mental health. Although most people are busy, it's important to take time to nourish yourself and treat yourself with the love and kindness you deserve.

"Your first relationship is with yourself and it's the foundation of relationships with others. Loving yourself enables you to live in alignment with your values and to make healthy choices in your everyday decisions. Confidence, self-respect, self-worth, and self-love are all interconnected. As we deepen in love for ourselves, we can deepen the love we share with others."[15]

I began practicing daily self-affirmations, which is the act of affirming one's own worthiness and value as an individual for beneficial effect (such as increasing one's confidence or raising self-esteem).

I began to understand how you start your day is how you live your day, and I committed to live in peace. I started to wake up every morning and look into the mirror and say, "You are the man. Today will be a great day. You will succeed at every task presented. You already won, live your life freely. Have faith over fear and peace over stress. You are more than enough."

Additionally, I added gospel music to my morning routine, which enriched my soul. The messages in gospel music were what my heart longed for, such as: "You're the God of miracles, we believe in your power" or "You did the impossible" or "You thought I was to die for, so You sacrificed your life, so I can be free" or "You give me joy, down deep in my soul" or "My God is amazing."

In January 2023, my wife and I became members of a different church located in Upper Marlboro, Maryland. We

---

15   https://www.verywellmind.com/ways-to-practice-self-love-5667417

regularly attended Sunday church services and events with our kids and routinely paid tithes.

I realized I needed to be more intentional in devoting time to read the Bible, which strengthens my faith, brings me closer to God, and gives me joy and appreciation for how blessed I am. I learned to read the Bible to get a heart for God and not just as a habit. Certain scriptures blessed me such as, "Now faith is the substance of things hoped for, the evidence of things not seen" (Hebrews 11:1, New King James Version) as well as "And such trust have we through Christ to God-ward: Not that we are sufficient of ourselves to think any thing as of ourselves; but our sufficiency is of God;" (2 Corinthians 3:4-5, King James Version).[16]

I also started to practice yoga multiple days a week. Medical News Today defines yoga as, "A mind and body practice that can build strength and flexibility. It may also help manage pain and reduce stress. Various styles of yoga combine physical postures, breathing, techniques, and meditation.

"Yoga maintains that chakras are center points of energy, thoughts, feelings, and the physical body.

"According to yogic teachers, chakras determine how people experience reality through emotional reactions, desires or aversions, levels of confidence of fear, and even physical

---

16   The Holy Bible, Bible App, Life Church, 2008

symptoms and effects. When energy becomes blocked in a chakra, it triggers physical, mental, or emotional imbalances that manifest in symptoms such as anxiety, lethargy, or poor digestion."[17]

Yoga helped me focus on my mindfulness and being present in the moment throughout my day. We are prone to focusing on "what's next," whether short-term or long-term. Yoga helped me train my mind to "stay in the present." I stopped worrying about the future and things I couldn't control.

Life will pass you by if you constantly worry all the time. A lot of times we think we are enjoying ourselves in the present, but we are fooling ourselves because we never remain in the present. Our minds are conditioned to leave the present and focus on what's next.

It had been nearly a year since I posted the last video talking about my stuttering journey, but now invigorated with my daily affirmations and yoga lifestyle, I was again led to make and post another video.

I posted a video to Instagram and Facebook with the caption *The Journey!* I know these social media apps are usually used to show our highlights in life, but it's also good to encourage others through sharing your personal journey and

---

17   https://www.medicalnewstoday.com/articles/286745

struggles and how you got through them. I didn't write anything down; I spoke directly from the heart.

During part of the video I said, "I was diagnosed as a person who stutters at the age of seven. As a kid I didn't go to
speech therapy, and I didn't meet any kids that also stuttered,
so as I was going through grade school, I always felt alone.

"It was at the point where sometimes as a kid, I would
pray that my stutter was like a bad headache, that I would fall
asleep, wake up in the morning and my stutter would be gone,
but of course that was not the case. So, as a kid, and even into
adulthood, I never accepted stuttering because I never talked
about it with anybody.

"Fast forward to a few years ago. I went to speak to a
therapist. I was having some anxiety because my career was
progressing pretty fast, so I sat down with the therapist and
we were talking through some things and he asked, 'Do you
realize you haven't talked about your career, parenthood, or
marriage? You have only talked about your stuttering.'

"So, I removed that fear because, as we know, fear can
be paralyzing, right, and I joined what's called the National
Stuttering Association, and I can tell you this: it has completely transformed my life. It is one of the best decisions I have
ever made. I have learned that I'm called a covert stutterer.
It's a person who knows how to maneuver around their stutter

and do things like word replacements; replace words that you struggle with to get through certain situations.

"Anyway, I made this video because we have to love ourselves more. We're our biggest critics, right, and I'm a person who's naturally humble and modest. When folks say nice things about me, it makes me uncomfortable, but I'm changing my mindset. I'm going to start to accept those things. I'm talking about self-affirmations. Every day I wake up now and say, 'You are the man, you can accomplish anything.' If I have a big meeting or a briefing, before I do it, I say, 'You are going to kill this briefing,' so it's about loving and appreciating ourselves more."

The video had nearly 600 views and over fifty comments. I also received direct messages regarding how people appreciated my vulnerability and transparency. One direct message in particular touched my soul. The message stated, "Thank you for being vulnerable. I think I need to see a therapist. My mental health is not good, but I'm embarrassed and worried about what other people will think. For you to post on social media for the world to see that you went to see a therapist is inspiring. You are courageous and a true example; you helped me today. I want you to know that I scheduled an appointment with a therapist after watching your video ten times; I kept replaying it. Thank you."

In the spring of 2023, I decided I wanted to post a series of motivational videos on Instagram and Facebook. I had just received a Distinguished Service Award for Innovation and Outstanding Leadership from Agency 4, which was a great honor. I was sitting in my house one day and I came up with "MTripleI", which is an acronym for "Motivate, Inspire, Influence and Impact." I realized I had a God-given talent, and it needed to be shared with the world or, in my case, the people I was connected to.

I structured the videos toward things like gratitude and the general happiness that we all desire and deserve. I also focused on maintaining our happiness and shifting our mindsets from thinking every single thing that happens to us is a crisis, and that although change is difficult for most people, it's inevitable and constant. So, shifting our mind from focusing on what we've lost, we have to think about how change can positively influence our lives.

Thousands of people worldwide viewed this series of videos. I realized I had to take my social pages off the private settings to reach more viewers and I hash tagged—#MTripleI #motivate #inspire #impact #influence—in every video because some viewers search for content by hashtag.

In July 2023, the NSA scheduled their annual conference in Fort Lauderdale, FL, and I registered to attend. I was so excited. I had only heard great things from the NSA DC chapter's members, some of whom had been going yearly for a long time. The conference started on a Wednesday with registration and welcome events, but on Thursday it really got going. I flew into Fort Lauderdale early Thursday morning, checked into my hotel room, and made it in time to attend one of the first workshops of the day. I was immediately inspired.

When they gave the audience an opportunity to speak, I volunteered, and I talked for a couple of minutes, but I remember specifically saying, "I have turned into this person whose purpose is to inspire. I now post videos on social media and for those of us who stutter, the hardest thing is to see and hear ourselves stutter. These posts not only inspire other people, but I inspire myself in the process because it takes bravery and courage to do those things as a person who stutters.

"I have folks who stutter and those who do not stutter that comment on my page saying 'thank you for doing this, it takes courage for you to be vulnerable and to show yourself stuttering on camera.' In most of my posts, I'm talking about self-love. Right? Self-love is so important because we beat ourselves up so often, so it's important to do self-affirmations. Every day I wake up and tell myself, 'you are the man,' and I always say 'you are more than enough.'"

Many people in the workshop resonated with what I was saying.

Throughout the conference, I attended several workshops and engaged in very interesting conversations and enjoyed the experience. Every day there was an "Open Mic" workshop, where those in the room could say whatever was on their mind. I made it a point to attend every open mic workshop; not always to speak, but to learn and hear how I have shared the same experiences as others. Over 500 people of all ages, races, and backgrounds attended the conference.

During the keynote presentations, when all conference attendees were in the same room, I stood in the back of the room, just to take it all in. Standing there, I looked left to right, scanning the room in awe as tears of joy flowed down my face. I started to reflect on how much of my life I felt alone with my stuttering, and now I was in a room with over 500 people who stuttered, and it was beautiful.

CHAPTER 17

My Son Stutters

I never went through life worrying about if my kids would stutter. For most of my life, I was so focused on not stuttering, the possibility never occurred to me that one of my future children might stutter. Only my great-grandfather on my father's side of the family stuttered. Other than him, there was not a family history of people who stuttered.

News Medical's discussion on genetic factors in stuttering disorders states, "According to the latest research in genetics, hereditary stuttering can occur in several generations in a family. In this case, congenital stuttering is observed in cases where the child's speech apparatus is weakened due to inherited genetic factors.

"Scientists and members of the American Speech-Language-Hearing Association believe that many stutterers inherit certain traits that put them at risk for developing this speech disorder. The exact nature of these traits is currently not fully understood, but they impair a person's ability to link muscle movements necessary for a smooth and free pronunciation of phrases into a single chain."[18]

"Representatives of the American Association for Speech, Language, and Hearing suggest that many people who have some speech impairment inherit certain traits, such as weak central speech mechanisms. However, this is not a reason for pessimism, because, despite the presence of certain links between stuttering and genetics, one must also remember that genetically inherited pathology manifests itself only in the presence of additional negative factors.

"American scientists from the National Institute for Deafness and Speech Disorders conducted research in which they found substantial evidence that stuttering can be inherited. In the process of studying the problem, the researchers found a strong connection on the long arm of the 12th chromosome. The results were obtained from a control group of Pakistani relatives who suffered from stuttering. Several unrelated families from Pakistan, North America, and the United Kingdom were also analyzed.

"The twin method, carried out by the same group of scientists, showed that in identical twins, who passed on the

18   https://www.news-medical.net/health/The-Genetic-Factors-in-Stuttering-Disorders.aspx

same number of identical genes, both children will stutter in 20–63% of cases."

When my son DC2 was in preschool, he started exhibiting minor signs of stuttering, and then it seemed as if it went away during kindergarten, which the first half of the kindergarten school year was virtual learning because of the global pandemic.

Once DC2 entered 1st grade in 2022, the stuttering appeared to have returned and became more recognizable to his mom and I. During a quarterly parent teacher conference, we asked his teacher whether she had observed DC2 stuttering in class, and she stated "No", but she recommended if we were concerned to request a consultation with the school's speech-language pathologist.

We scheduled the meeting, and DC2 had his one-on-one speech evaluation. A week later, the speech pathologist called us and stated during DC2's session she noticed normal fluency for his age. We explained we noticed signs of disfluency, specifically stuttering at home. She told us to just keep an eye out for it, but in her opinion, he does not have disfluency.

At seven years old, when DC2 entered 2nd grade, his stuttering increased, and he started exhibiting struggling behaviors. For example, he would stomp his foot during conversations and also state "it won't come out" when trying to say certain words, and became more frustrated while speaking. I started asking DC2 how he feels when he speaks and if it is hard to speak sometimes and he said, "Yes, and I don't know why." I asked DC2 if he noticed that I also struggle at times when speaking and sometimes stretch words and repeat words while speaking and he responded, "Yes, he does notice it."

I decided it was time to take DC2 to a pediatric speech and language pathology center to have him thoroughly evaluated and scheduled the appointment in December 2023. On the way there, he was really inquisitive and wanted to know what he was going to do at this appointment.

That was the first time I explained to him my interpretation of stuttering. I told him, "We are going to get you evaluated for stuttering. You know when I struggle to say certain words, I repeat them or stretch the word out, like 'cacacacar,' that's stuttering. It's a speech disorder that I have, and we believe you also have it.

"The specialist is going to ask you some questions and also have you say some words and phrases. It's going to be pretty easy. I was your age when my mom took me to get a speech evaluation for stuttering."

DC2 wasn't fully aware of his stutter yet. He had just started exhibiting signs of frustration at this point. When I was his age, I was aware of my stutter and had been for a while, and it had already started bothering me.

My wife and I attended the evaluation with DC2. Once we entered the room, DC2 sat down in the chair; he was shy at first, but the specialist made him very comfortable. We observed from the corner of the room, while DC2 engaged with the specialist. The evaluation lasted a little over an hour. In the end, the specialist confirmed DC2 did stutter, and highly recommended speech therapy.

She let us know she would send a full report in a week's time so we could provide it to a speech therapist if we decided that's the course of action we were planning to pursue. After the appointment, I immediately started researching adolescent speech therapists in my area. My initial thought was not that speech therapy would eliminate his stutter; that's a myth. I truly believed it would help him manage it and get an early start on his self-acceptance so he could live his life with the confidence to speak freely in spite of stuttering. That is what I was missing as a kid, and I wanted to give DC2 that opportunity.

I felt relieved when DC2 was officially diagnosed as a person who stutters, and I was ready to support him in every way possible. I also wanted to normalize stuttering with DC2 and our family. Having a negative connotation, stuttering was always a big secret and never talked about with me as a kid.

I ordered us matching T-shirts that read, "Yes, I stutter, no, my IQ is not lower than yours. Surely, I know what I want to say. No, I'm not shy. No, you shouldn't interrupt me to complete my sentences." DC2 was as equally excited to wear the T-shirts as I was.

Positive and uplifting, it was a great introduction to stuttering for DC2. This small act showed him he should never feel ashamed of stuttering. I was DC2's hero and him seeing me proudly wearing the T-shirt made him feel proud, too. We took pictures in the T-shirts, and it was amazing, one of the best days of my life.

I wrote DC2 a letter and read it to him out loud. As a person who stutters and the parent of a person who stutters, I cried while reading the letter to him because it meant the world to me to share this with him. He didn't fully understand the impact and message in the letter at seven years old, but when he gets older, he will.

I posted the pictures of us in matching shirts to my Instagram and Facebook pages with the letter to DC2 as the caption which stated, "Dear DC2, I got you, son. As you navigate life as a person who stutters, I'm going to be right there with you. You have nothing to fear. God created you and me in His own image, just like all mankind, except we talk a little differently. Four years ago, when I joined the National Stuttering Association, I began my journey of accepting my stuttering, which was long overdue. I also started to finally remove the feelings of embarrassment and self-doubt.

"I didn't know God was preparing me to be a motivator and someone who inspires others through the transparency with my stuttering journey. I realize, most importantly, God was preparing me to lead and guide you through your stuttering journey and man, I am so honored and excited.

"I can't promise you that you will never be embarrassed, never be made fun of, or never have self-doubt, but when you do, I will be right there to guide you through it and provide you with every tool and resource to overcome (succeed while dealing with your stutter) so you can achieve whatever your heart desires in life. Love Dad!"

DC2 started speech therapy in January 2024, and the speech therapist took the first couple of sessions to teach DC2 about stuttering, which I thought was very important. I saw the benefits of speech therapy immediately. He enjoyed it, which was a pleasant surprise. He learned the different types of stuttering: prolongations, sentence repetitions, part-word repetitions, whole word repetitions, phrase repetition, and blocks.

Not only did he learn the names but also the definitions and taught me things about stuttering that I was unaware of. He would even call out the types of stuttering that I was doing, "Daddy you just had a block, Daddy you just had a part-word repetition." It was pretty amazing and inspiring that he was so comfortable with his stuttering and was becoming more confident.

He came home from school one day and said, "Daddy, my classmate asked me 'why I talk like that,' and I told her, 'I stutter, it's a speech disorder.'" I remember being asked that question at eight years old and I would freeze up. I wasn't confident enough to even respond, so I was proud of him for speaking up for himself and also educating his classmates.

I was also happy that he felt comfortable enough to talk to me about his stuttering and that his mom and I had created a safe space for him and his sibling to express how they feel. DC2 also learned strategies to help with stuttering at speech therapy, and what I observed was the strategies wouldn't always reduce his stuttering, but the strategies did help reduce the frustration, and stress that stuttering causes because most importantly he learned immediately after he was diagnosed as a person who stutters that, "It's ok to stutter."

One of the co-leaders of the NSA DC Chapter informed me that there were several stuttering organizations that catered specifically to kids, like FRIENDS (The National Association of Young People Who Stutter) and SAY (The Stuttering Association for The Young). I visited their websites and followed their social media pages to form a connection and look into future events for DC2 and I to attend.

The co-chapter leader informed me that in June 2024, FRIENDS was hosting a one-day conference in the DC area and that if I was interested, he would like for my son and me to attend and for me to participate as a panelist during the conference and share my experience as a person who stutters and a parent of a person who stutters. I immediately stated, "We will be there, and I would love to sit on the panel."

I was super excited for DC2 to meet other kids who stuttered, something I never experienced as a child. The day of the conference was a beautiful, sunny Saturday in June. DC2 and I arrived at the conference to check in. There were 100 people at the conference, which was a great turnout for a one-day conference. The conference had breakout groups for kids and adults in the morning.

An amazing conversation, complete with laughter and tears, took place while I was in one of the adult breakout groups. I shared my unique perspective as a person who stutters and a parent of person who stutters and how excited I was to walk along the journey with DC2 and give him the resources and connection to the stuttering community that I never had. Some parents didn't share my excitement because they were concerned about the difficulties their children were experiencing.

They were also concerned because this was new for them, because they didn't stutter. Unlike me, they had no experience with stuttering, and their children were young, just like DC2. They really didn't know what to do and felt helpless. I told them, "Just by you being here today, you are already going down the correct path.

"Your child meeting other kids who stutter will have amazing benefits in their development and confidence. My advice is to support them and allow them to dictate their own path. If you put them in speech therapy and they don't like it, they shouldn't be made to go. If they don't want to come to anymore stuttering events, then so be it. What's important is your child needs to know it's ok to stutter and you have to provide them with a safe home environment where they are not afraid to speak up and express how they feel."

Mid-morning, I walked past the kids' breakout session and heard tons of laughter and exuberance, and I was very pleased. It was awesome that FRIENDS made the kids' environment informative, but most importantly, fun. I specifically heard DC2's voice loud and clear. He was thoroughly enjoying himself.

After lunch, we had a panel discussion, with all attendees present, and I was joined on stage by three other individuals who also stuttered. We introduced ourselves and then we all got an opportunity to respond to questions from the moderators. The hour-long panel discussion was remarkable. Afterward, several parents came up to me and thanked me for sharing my story, insights, and showing kids that confidence and stuttering can co-exist.

I didn't share my social media handles with anyone at the conference, but one parent found me on Instagram and sent me a message stating, "Thank you so much for sharing your story. My son talked the whole ride home about how good it felt to be in a room with people who stutter but, more importantly, people who looked like him and were confident in their stutter.

"He wasn't sold on the idea of coming to the conference, but was open to giving it a try. NOW he's so hopeful, inspired, and may even want to come to the bigger conferences … I'm still working on him with that one. Continue to share your story. People are listening."

That message touched my soul because although I'm inspiring adults, children are who I most want to inspire and impact. I remember being seven years old and thinking, "I won't be able to do anything when I grow up because I stutter." Now I have become a successful and confident stutterer, and I need to continue being a shining example to children who stutter and give them something to aspire to and go way beyond what I have accomplished.

As I reflect, I try to always remember what the doctor told me and my wife before DC2's birth when he was born severely premature. I thank God everyday that DC2 and I can share our stuttering journeys together because, in an alternate universe, he could have never made it out of the NICU alive.

CHAPTER 18

The Confident Stutterer

I discovered that my thoughts and beliefs had a deep influence on my speech pattern and, by changing my thinking, I could change the way I behaved and approached everyday life. I finally started seeing my stutter as a strength, not a weakness and by doing so, I became happier, less stressed, and more confident. I also adopted a mindset of peace and gratitude for how good God had been to me.

Also, through practicing yoga, and the mind-body connection between stuttering and the impact of stress because of my stutter, I learned to manage my stress and anxiety through mindfulness and positive self-talk. I also leaned into my stuttering more than ever. I embraced it, loved it, and openly spoke about it to build my self-esteem and, most importantly, conquered my fear. I finally became a confident stutterer, something I never imagined achieving, and I was loving myself more than ever.

We have to face our fears head on. When we are afraid of something, whether it's a fear or spiders, snakes, or public speaking, it can be tempting to avoid it. I know it's a cliché and overused, but it's essential to the development of every human being. Avoidance may give us relief in the short term, but can make things we fear harder to overcome in the long run. Instead, we have to gradually expose ourselves to the situations or things we fear, so we can start to slowly, but surely, overcome them and feel more in control.

I was once asked the question, "Do you have more anxiety preparing for a presentation, doing the presentation, or after the presentation?" For me, it was always the preparation phase. During the presentation and after, I had the feeling of satisfaction. My father-in-law gave me some sound, but simple advice, and it was a method he used when he had to do briefings or presentations for high-level officials.

He always told himself, "This day too shall pass" which meant regardless of how the briefing went, he was going to go home to his family and have more opportunities in the future. It wasn't the end of the world, and he should never approach a situation with that attitude.

I was also asked the question, "How did you become a confident stutterer?" My response was, "I leaned into my bright and vibrant personality, which I had suppressed much of my life due to fear and avoidance because of my stutter. I realized allowing my personality to show was important to me. Being a positive and confident speaker helped conversations flow naturally and helped me connect with people. I also allowed my genuineness and passion for whatever I was speaking about permeate my audiences and, most importantly, I learned to stutter openly and freely, and I let my infectious personality and positivity show."

Positive self-talk raised my confidence to the next level. Gradually removing the negative self-talk and insecurities surrounding my stuttering from my daily life was essential to becoming a confident stutterer and speaker in general.

Also, removing the mental health stigma which really originates from a lack of understanding, fear, and the negative views of those who suffer from mental health issues helped me as well. Therapy and joining a stuttering organization put me on a path of positive self-talk and completely changed my life and how I viewed myself as a person who stutters.

If you get anything from this book, I pray you understand that you are "more than enough"; you have the power to control how you perceive yourself, the ability to silence the negative voice, empower the positive voice, and love yourself unconditionally to unleash your true potential so you can achieve whatever your heart desires.

Citations

1. "Stuttering." National Institute on Deafness and Other Communication Disorders, last modified March 6, 2017, https://www.nidcd.nih.gov/health/stuttering#what.

2. "What Is Stuttering." National Stuttering Association, accessed June 4, 2024, https://westutter.org/what-is-stuttering/.

3. "Suitable for 2–8 years Stuttering." Raising Children Network (Australia), last updated May 15, 2022, https://raisingchildren.net.au/preschoolers/development/language-development/stuttering.

4. Red, Merk, "Joning." Urban Dictionary, December 20, 2005, https://www.urbandictionary.com/define.php?term=Joning

5. Zauderer, Steven, "31 Fear of Public Speaking Statistics (Prevalence)." Cross River Therapy, September 19, 2023, https://www.crossrivertherapy.com/public-speaking-statistics#sources.

6. Meyer, Jean and Lauren Provus, "Covert Stuttering: I've Got a Secret-and It's Scaring Me to Death!" Minnesota State University, accessed June 8, 2024, https://ahn.mnsu.edu/services-and-centers/center-for-communication-sciences-and-disorders/services/stuttering/information-about-stuttering/serious-information/types-of-fluency-disorders/covert-stuttering/covert-stuttering-ive-got-a-secret--and-its-scaring-me-to-death/.

7. "Black Mental Health: What You Need To Know." Mass General Brigham McLean, last updated July 15, 2024, https://www.mcleanhospital.org/essential/black-mental-health.

8. Saymeh, Amal, MBA, "What is imposter syndrome? Definition, symptoms, and overcoming it." BetterUp, February 22, 2023, https://www.betterup.com/blog/what-is-imposter-syndrome-and-how-to-avoid-it

9. Tee-Melegrito, Rachel Ann, "What to know about self-loathing," medically reviewed by Vara Saripalli, Psy.D. MedicalNewsToday, October 4, 2022, https://www.medicalnewstoday.com/articles/self-loathing.

10. "NSA's 41st Annual Conference." National Stuttering Association, accessed June 18, 2024, https://westutter.org/.

11. "How to deal with emotional pain: 8 ways to support yourself," clinically reviewed by Dr. Chris Mosunic, PhD, RD, CCES, MBA. Calm, accessed June 20, 2024, https://www.calm.com/blog/emotional-pain.

12. Oshinkale, Yetunde, "Definition of Mentorship: What is a Mentor and Do You Need One?" World Education Services, September 18, 2019, https://www.wes.org/advisor-blog/definition-of-mentorship/.

13. Field, Barbara. "7 Ways to Practice Self-Love," reviewed by Ivy Kwong, LMFT. Verywell Mind, September 30, 2022, https://www.verywellmind.com/ways-to-practice-self-love-5667417.

14. *The Holy Bible*, Bible App, Life Church, 2008, accessed July 1, 2024.

15. Nichols, Hannah. "How does yoga work?" medically reviewed by Courtney Sullivan, Certified Yoga Instructor. Medical News Today, updated April 26, 2023, https://www.medicalnewstoday.com/articles/286745.

16. Dorofeev, Dmitry, B.Sc, "The Genetic Factors in Stuttering Disorders," reviewed by Sophia Coveney. News Medical Life Sciences, last updated April 27, 2022, https://www.news-medical.net/health/The-Genetic-Factors-in-Stuttering-Disorders.aspx.

About the Author

DaVon B. Camp was born and raised in Washington, DC, and currently serves as a Hotline Director at a Federal Government Agency. In addition to being a mentor and stuttering advocate, he's a husband and father of four children.

DaVon was diagnosed as a person who stutters at the age of seven and spent much of his life feeling alone and ashamed of his stuttering. It wasn't until he found the National Stuttering Association at age thirty-five, that he finally accepted his stuttering, turned it into his biggest strength, and no longer considered his speech a weakness.

DaVon's purpose in life is to show his son, who also stutters—and all people who stutter—that confidence and stuttering, two words that are never mentioned together, can co-exist. He also wants to inspire and motivate all people who struggle with self-doubt and insecurities to love their flaws with a great deal of intention, compassion, and patience.

Visit davoncamp.com to order books, book DaVon to speak, or to connect with the author.

Connect and Share

If you enjoyed *Stuttering to the Top,* please leave a review of the book on the site where you purchased it and order copies for others who may be inspired by the author's story. Connect with DaVon B. Camp online:

davoncamp.com
Instagram.com/dcdavon
Facebook.com: DaVon Camp

www.ingramcontent.com/pod-product-compliance
Lightning Source LLC
Chambersburg PA
CBHW071005120626
46546CB00003B/947